CAVENDISH
LawCards®

## Evidence

GW00514844

Cavendish
Publishing
Limited

First published in Great Britain 1998 by Cavendish Publishing Limited, The Glass House, Wharton Street, London WC1X 9PX, United Kingdom

Telephone: +44 (0) 171 278 8000 Facsimile: +44 (0) 171 278 8080

e-mail: info@cavendishpublishing.com

Visit our Home Page on http://www.cavendishpublishing.com

Lawcard on evidence

1 Evidence (Law) – England 2 Evidence (Law) –Wales

345.4'206

ISBN 1 85941 428 1

Printed and bound in Great Britain

# Contents

# 1 Introduction

## Basic concepts

### Definition of 'evidence'

The meaning of 'evidence' depends to some extent on context, but the word is often used to refer to any matter of fact, the effect, tendency or design of which is to produce in the mind a persuasion of the existence or non-existence of some other matter of fact.

### Relevance

'Relevance' refers to the relationship that exists between an item of evidence and a fact that has to be proved, which makes the matter requiring proof more or less probable. In the vast majority of cases, it is not the law that determines whether an item of evidence is relevant, but logic and general experience. General experience will often be expressed as a generalisation about the way things are in the world. The burden is on the party who tenders evidence to show its relevance; it is not for the party challenging relevance to show that the evidence in question is irrelevant (*R v Bracewell* (1978)). Relevance is important for the law of evidence because:

- irrelevant evidence is inadmissible (*R v Turner* (1975));

- the way in which an item of evidence is relevant may govern its admissibility (for example, hearsay, similar fact evidence).

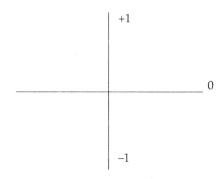

The probability or otherwise of what one party to litigation alleges can be expressed in the diagram above. The point +1 represents the mental condition of being certain that what the party alleges is true; -1 represents certainty that the allegation is untrue. Any item of evidence making it more or less likely that that the allegation is true will have a place on the scale at some point between 0 and +1, or between 0 and -1, and will, in principle, be relevant at trial. Note that an item of evidence does not have to be conclusive to be relevant. Questions of relevance generally depend on the individual circumstances of each case (*R v Guney* (1998)). But a judge may decide that something that is relevant according to ordinary reasoning is not legally relevant. This may be the case, for example, where a judge wishes to avoid a proliferation of side issues that may confuse a jury or give rise to mere speculation (*Hollingham v Head* (1858); *R v Blastland* (1986)).

## Weight

The 'weight' of an item of evidence refers to the extent to which that item makes a proposition more or less probable. In the diagram above, it is relevance that gets an item of evidence onto the scale in the first place, but it is weight that governs the position that it takes there. The 'weightier' the evidence, the nearer it will be to one or other extremity. Where the judicial function is split between a judge and a jury, questions of relevance are decided by the judge, and questions of weight by the jury. But a judge sometimes makes decisions about weight, for example, where the defence ask that an item of prosecution evidence be excluded on the ground that its prejudicial effect outweighs its probative value, or where the judge has to rule on the admissibility of an item of 'similar fact' evidence.

Although relevance and weight are distinct concepts, there is some connection between them, because the weight of an item of evidence may be affected by the form of the generalisation that is relied on to support its relevance. The bolder the generalisation, the weightier the evidence is likelier to be. But a bold generalisation is less likely than a cautious one to be true. So where X is charged with the murder of Y, and it can be proved that X quarrelled with Y shortly before the latter's death, the relevance and weight of the fact of the quarrel might be considered as follows:

| Generalisation | Comment |
|---|---|
| (1) People who quarrel with others usually murder them. | If true, the evidence is relevant and weighty. But this generalisation is certainly false, and, unless a more acceptable generalisation can be found, the evidence must be irrelevant. |
| (2) Where a murder victim has quarrelled recently with someone, that person is more likely to be the culprit than someone who had not quarrelled recently with him. | A little more plausible. If true, evidence relevant and fairly weighty. |
| (3) Where a murder victim has recently had a quarrel with someone, that person may have had a motive for murder, and may be more likely to be the culprit than someone who had no motive. | Probably an acceptable generalisation, so the evidence of the quarrel is relevant, but it is too weak to be anything more than of very slight weight. |

### Admissibility

An item of evidence may be relevant and weighty, but inadmissible because of some rule of law. Where the judicial function is divided between a judge and a jury, decisions about admissibility are made by the judge.

## Basic terminology

### Best evidence rule

This was an old rule requiring that 'the best evidence must be given of which the nature of the thing is capable'. It did not require the greatest amount of evidence that could possibly be given of any fact. The object of the rule was to prevent the introduction of any evidence which, from the nature of the case, suggested that better evidence was in the possession of the party producing it. Thus, in *Chenie v Watson* (1797) oral evidence of the physical condition of certain objects was rejected because the objects themselves could have been produced in court. The rule is generally considered to have fallen into abeyance (*Garton v Hunter* (1969)).

### Circumstantial evidence

This expression refers to evidence of a fact that is not itself a fact in issue (see below), but is a fact from which the existence or non-existence of a fact in issue can be inferred.

### Direct evidence

Depending on the context, this expression may refer to evidence that is first hand rather than hearsay (see below), or to evidence of a fact in issue (see below) rather than circumstantial evidence (see above).

### Documentary evidence

This expression refers to evidence of the contents of documents, which include anything in which information of any description is recorded (Sched 2, para 5(1) of the Criminal Justice Act 1988, as amended, and s 13 of the Civil Evidence Act 1995), and may therefore include such items as films, tapes, and video recordings. Documentary evidence should not be confused with affidavit evidence, which is a form of testimony (see below).

**Facts in issue**
In civil actions this expression refers to those facts alleged in the pleadings, including facts necessary to establish pleaded defences, that are either denied or not admitted by the other party. In criminal cases the effect of a plea of 'not guilty' is to make everything that the substantive law makes material to the offence a fact in issue (*R v Sims* (1946)).

**Hearsay**
The effect of the rule against hearsay is that an assertion other than one made by a person while giving oral evidence in the proceedings is inadmissible as evidence of any fact asserted (*R v Sharp* (1988)). See further, below, Chapter 6.

**Original evidence**
Depending on context, this expression can refer to evidence that is first hand, in the sense that it does not come before the tribunal at second hand or in some other derivative way; alternatively, the expression can refer to evidence of words uttered by someone other than the testifying witness, where the object is not to prove the truth of the words uttered, but merely the fact that the utterance was made.

**Real evidence**
This expression refers to items of evidence that are presented to the senses of the tribunal and may be examined by it.

**Testimony**
This expression refers to an oral or written statement of facts, made on oath or affirmation, and used for the purpose

of legal proceedings. A written statement of facts made in these circumstances is called 'an affidavit'.

### Voir dire

The voir dire is a trial within a trial, in which the court determines disputed facts that have to be established before certain items of evidence, such as a confession, can be admitted.

## Functions of judge and jury

In jury trials the judicial function is divided between the judge, whose decision on matters of law is (subject to a right of appeal) final, and the jury, who are in principle the sole judges of fact. Every summing up should contain a direction to the jury about these separate functions (*R v Jackson* (1992)). It is particularly important that the division of functions be made clear to the jury, because the law permits the trial judge to comment on the evidence in his summing up (*R v Sparrow* (1973)), although the judge should not go so far as to give his own views about whether or not a witness has told the truth (*R v Iroegbu* (1988)).

But note that a judge in a criminal trial may have to make rulings about facts, for example:

- where it is necessary to establish the existence of certain facts (such as those required to establish a witness' competence to testify, or the admissibility of a confession) before a particular witness' evidence, or a particular item of evidence, can be admitted;

- where the defence submit that there is no case to answer (*R v Galbraith* (1981)).

Although the judge's directions on the law are his responsibility, it has become increasingly common for judges to invite prosecution and defence advocates to address them on the content of those directions where there is room for more than one view about what they should be, and in *R v Higgins* (1995) the Court of Appeal suggested that counsel has a duty to raise appropriate matters before closing speeches without waiting to be asked by the judge.

# 2 Competence and compellability

Competence has as its subject matter the persons *permitted* by law to give evidence. Compellability has as its subject matter the persons who may be *compelled* by law to give evidence. The basic rule is that all persons are competent and compellable to give evidence (*Ex p Fernandez* (1861)), but there are special rules for four types of witnesses.

## Defendants in criminal cases

All defendants are competent, but not compellable, witnesses in their own defence, or in the defence of a co-accused (s 1 of the Criminal Evidence Act 1898).

An accused person is incompetent as a witness for the prosecution (s 1 of the Criminal Evidence Act 1898). Where two or more persons are charged and the prosecution want to use the evidence of one against the others, it is necessary to separate that person from his companions so that he ceases to be their co-accused. This may be done by:

* discontinuing proceedings against the potential witness;

* obtaining a separate trial for the potential witness;

* obtaining a plea of guilty from the potential witness before trial of his companions.

Where a defendant gives evidence at his own trial, he must do so on oath or affirmation and will be liable to cross-examination (s 72 of the Criminal Justice Act 1972). His testimony will be evidence at the trial *for all purposes*. Thus, he may incriminate himself in the witness box, and anything he says there may be used as evidence against any co-defendant (*R v Rudd* (1948)). Counsel for the prosecution is entitled to cross-examine with a view to incriminating him or any co-defendant (*R v Paul* (1920)). He may also be cross-examined on behalf of any co-defendant.

If a defendant fails to give evidence in his own defence (or, when giving evidence, refuses without good cause to answer any question) the court or jury, in determining whether he is guilty of the offence charged, may draw such inferences from that failure as appear proper (s 35 of the Criminal Justice and Public Order Act 1994). For this provision to apply, the defendant must:

- be over the age of 14 (s 35(1));
- have pleaded not guilty (s 35(1));
- be physically and mentally fit to testify (s 35(1));
- be aware of the risks attached to silence (s 35(2)).

If the case is one where a jury would be entitled to draw an inference under s 35, the judge must direct them in his summing up that:

- the burden of proof remains on the prosecution;
- the defendant is entitled to remain silent;
- the jury must be satisfied there is a case to answer before drawing any inferences from silence;
- the jury cannot convict solely on an inference drawn from silence;
- no inference is to be drawn unless the jury are sure that there is no other reasonable explanation, consistent with innocence, to account for the defendant's silence.

See *R v Cowan* (1997).

Similarly, a defendant in a civil case who chooses not to testify runs the risk that his silence, in circumstances where he would be expected to answer, might convert slight evidence against him into proof (*Gibbs v Rea* (1998)).

## Spouses of defendants in criminal cases

The rules are set out as follows in s 80 of the Police and Criminal Evidence Act 1984 (PACE):

- the accused's spouse is, subject to sub-s (4), always competent for the prosecution (s 80(1)(a));

- the accused's spouse is always competent for the accused and competent for someone jointly charged with the accused (s 80 (1)(b));

- the accused's spouse is always, subject to sub-s (4), compellable for the accused (s 80(2));

- the accused's spouse is, subject to sub-s (4), compellable for the prosecution only where:

  ○ the offence charged involves an assault on, or injury or a threat of injury to, the spouse of the accused or a person who was at the material time under the age of 16; or

  ○ the offence charged is a sexual offence alleged to have been committed in respect of a person who was at the material time under the age of 16; or

  ○ the offence charged consists of attempting or conspiring to commit either of the above, or being a secondary party to or inciting either of the above (s 80(3)).

Sub-s (4) provides that where a husband and wife are jointly charged with an offence, neither spouse shall at the trial be competent or compellable by virtue of sub-ss (1)(a), (2) or (3) to give evidence in respect of that offence unless that spouse is not, or is no longer, liable to be convicted of that offence at the trial, whether as a result of pleading guilty or for any other reason.

The accused's spouse is compellable for a co-accused only in those circumstances where he or she would be compellable for the prosecution (s 80(3)).

In any proceedings a person who has been, but is no longer, married to the accused shall be competent and compellable to give evidence as if that person and the accused had never been married (s 80(5)).

Two main problems have arisen in the interpretation of s 80:

(a) s 80(3)(a) clearly covers offences, such as robbery or rape, where violence or the threat of it is an essential part of the *actus reus*. But it is unclear whether 'involves' covers an offence where this is not the case, and the violence is only an incidental element;

(b) in *R v Woolgar* (1991) the Court of Appeal held that 'jointly charged' in sub-s (3) meant *jointly charged with an offence* and not merely *jointly indicted*. But if this is right:

- it appears that the compellability of a spouse for a co-defendant is still governed by the common law, and not the Act; and

- it creates problems for the interpretation of 'any person jointly charged with the accused' in sub-s (1).

## Children

### Civil cases

A child may give sworn evidence if it can satisfy the test in
*R v Hayes* (1977): does the child understand:

- the solemnity of the occasion; and

- the special duty to tell the truth, over and above the
  ordinary social duty to do so?

If the child does not satisfy these conditions, it may be able
to give evidence under s 96 of the Children Act 1989. By this
section, a child (any person under 18: see s 105) who does
not understand the nature of an oath may give unsworn
evidence if:

- he understands that it is his duty to speak the truth; and

- he has sufficient understanding to justify his evidence
  being heard.

## Summary

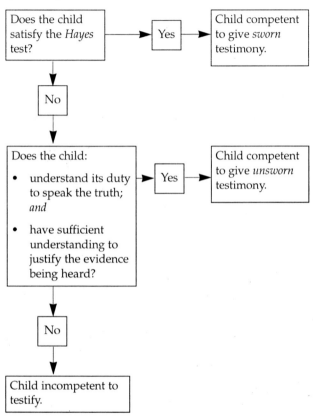

**Figure 2.1**

**Criminal cases**

The basic rules are contained in the Criminal Justice Act 1988, as amended, but note that a 'child' for these purposes means a person under 14 (s 33A). Children over 14 will be treated as if they were adults, and so will usually give sworn evidence without inquiry as to competency.

A child's evidence in criminal proceedings shall be given unsworn (s 33A(1)).

A child's evidence shall be received unless it appears to the court that the child is incapable of giving intelligible testimony (s 33A(2A)). Intelligible testimony is testimony that is capable of being understood (*G v DPP* (1997)). Expert evidence will not usually be admitted on this subject unless the child's ability to give intelligible evidence is affected by a medical condition (*G v DPP* (1997)). Where expert evidence is admissible on a question of competence, it should be heard on the voir dire in the absence of the jury (*R v Deakin* (1994)).

The judge retains a *power* to conduct a preliminary investigation of a child's competence, if he considers it necessary. Such an investigation should take place in open court, in the presence of the defendant, but not necessarily in the presence of the jury. The investigation should be conducted by the judge, and not through examination and cross-examination by counsel (*R v Hampshire* (1996)).

## Summary

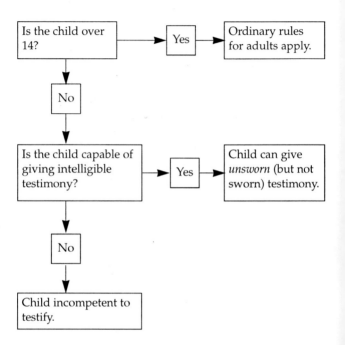

**Figure 2.2**

## Persons of defective intellect

Competence depends on the nature and severity of the disability, which may be investigated in open court before testimony is received. Expert evidence should be given on the voir dire to deal with the matter, but it should not normally be necessary to call the witness whose mental condition has given rise to the problem (*R v Barratt* (1996)).

The test to be applied is whether, despite any mental disability, the witness understands the nature of the oath in the light of the *Hayes* test (*R v Bellamy* (1985)).

# 3 The course of testimony

## Examination-in-chief

This is the first stage in the examination of a witness at trial, and is conducted on behalf of the party who has called him. In civil actions in the High Court, a witness' pre-trial written statement may stand as the evidence-in-chief (RSC Ord 38 r 2A(7)(a)), and the same may be ordered in county court hearings.

A witness will often be favourable to the cause of the party calling him. Because of this, two rules that are peculiar to examination-in-chief have developed: the rules against leading questions and against discrediting one's own witness.

### Rule against leading questions

A leading question is one that suggests to the witness the answer that is wanted. An advocate may not generally ask leading questions of his own witness on matters that are in contention, because such a witness is thought likely to agree to suggestions made to him on behalf of a person to whom the witness is probably favourable.

A less usual, but always illegitimate, form of leading question is one that assumes that something has already been established by evidence when that is not the case. In *Curtis v Peek* (1864), the issue was whether a particular custom existed. The witness had not yet given evidence of that fact. It was held improper to ask whether certain conduct was in accordance with the custom, because that question assumed the custom to exist.

## Rule against discrediting one's own witness

A witness called by a party should have been put forward on the basis that he is honest. If a witness' evidence unexpectedly turns out to be contrary to the interest of the party who has called him, the latter cannot repair the damage by trying to show that the witness is of bad character (*Wright v Beckett* (1834)). But the party who has called the witness may, in such a case, call other witnesses to contradict the damaging testimony (*Ewer v Ambrose* (1825)). He may also, in some circumstances, show that the witness has made previously a statement inconsistent with the testimony given (*Greenough v Eccles* (1859)).

## Cross-examination

The objects of cross-examination are to complete and correct the story told by a witness in examination-in-chief. Because of this, the right to cross-examine can be exercised by anyone whose interests have been affected by the testimony. Thus, co-plaintiffs and co-defendants may cross-examine each other (*Lord v Colvin* (1855); *R v Hadwen* (1902)). For the same reason, the scope of cross-examination is not confined to those matters dealt with during evidence-in-chief, but extends to all relevant matters (*Berwick-upon-Tweed Corpn v Murray* (1850)).

Because the witness who is cross-examined may be unfavourable to the party cross-examining, there is no reason for a rule against leading questions. Since the cross-examining party has not been responsible for bringing the witness before the court, he does not vouch for the witness' character, and so may discredit him by all the proper means at his disposal.

But evidence obtained by cross-examination must still be admissible under the ordinary rules of evidence. Thus, a defendant must not be cross-examined about evidence that is inadmissible in relation to the case against him, even though it may be admissible in relation to a co-defendant. In *R v Windass* (1989) it was held that a defendant should not have been asked questions in cross-examination about the contents of a co-defendant's diary, which had been written without any contribution from him. And in *R v Gray* (1998) it was held to be generally improper for the prosecution to cross-examine one defendant about the contents of a co-defendant's interview with the police.

### Cross-examining the police on other cases

It was held in *R v Edwards* (1991) that police officers should not be asked about:

- untried allegations of perjury made against them, or about complaints not yet ruled on by the Police Complaints Authority;

- discreditable conduct by other officers, whether or not in the same squad.

But an officer could be asked about a case involving a different defendant, in which the officer had given evidence and in which the defendant had been acquitted, *where that acquittal necessarily indicated that the jury had disbelieved the officer's testimony*. But in the absence of any reasons for a jury's verdict, this is an impossible test to satisfy. In *R v Meads* (1996) the Court of Appeal apparently approved a prosecutor's concession that defence cross-examination was permissible where a previous acquittal merely 'pointed to' fabrication of evidence by a police officer.

**Sexual Offences (Amendment) Act 1976**

The credibility of a witness is a relevant fact in any case because it is something that makes that witness' testimony about other relevant matters either more or less likely to be true. Cross-examination of a witness may be relevant either solely to credibility, or solely to an issue in the case, or to a mixture of both. For some centuries, moral character was regarded as relevant to credibility, and witnesses in any type of case could therefore be cross-examined about matters, including sexual habits, that were thought to reflect on their morality, and so on their credibility. The position was no different where a complainant alleged rape or a similar offence.

The Sexual Offences (Amendment) Act 1976 altered the common law to a limited extent. The Act applies where the defendant is charged with a 'rape offence', which includes rape, attempted rape, aiding and abetting rape or attempted rape, incitement to rape, conspiracy to rape, and burglary with intent to rape (s 7(2)). It does not include other sexual offences, such as indecent assault or unlawful sexual intercourse. But in relation to the latter it has been suggested that 'some of the considerations that concerned Parliament in rape cases apply' (*R v Funderburk* (1990)).

By s 2 of the Act, at the trial of a rape offence the defendant may not call any evidence, or ask any questions in cross-examination, about any sexual experience of the complainant with a person *other than the defendant* unless the judge gives leave. The judge shall give leave 'if and only if he is satisfied that it would be unfair to the defendant' to refuse.

The leading case in the interpretation of these provisions is *R v Viola* (1982), which held, *inter alia*, as follows:

- leave should be given if the evidence or questions might reasonably lead the jury to take a different view of the complainant's evidence. Once a judge has decided that he is satisfied that this is so, he must allow the evidence or questions;

- if the proposed line of questioning is designed merely to establish that because of the complainant's sexual behaviour she is not to be trusted on oath, leave should not be given. But if the questions or evidence are relevant to an issue in the trial in the light of the way the case is being run, they should be admitted;

- there is a grey area in such cases between relevance to credit and relevance to an issue in the case. Evidence of promiscuity may be so strong, or so contemporaneous with the event in issue, as to come to, or reach, the border between credit and issue. Conversely, relevant evidence might have such slight weight that it would not be unfair to exclude it.

Relevance is the key to the application of s 2. *R v Viola* was itself a case where the complainant's promiscuous behaviour over a period of hours was held relevant to the issue of consent. The complainant's sexual history may also become relevant because of her evidence of surrounding circumstances that gives a 'ring of truth' to her story as a whole. See, for example, *R v SMS* (1992); *R v Ellis* (1990).

### Cross-examination on previous inconsistent statements

A witness may be cross-examined about an earlier statement of his that is inconsistent with his testimony in court. In civil proceedings a previous inconsistent statement will be evidence of the truth of its contents (s 6(1) of the Civil

Evidence Act 1995), but this is not so in criminal proceedings. If a witness in a criminal case refuses to accept the truth of his earlier statement, the jury should be directed that it does not contain evidence on which they can act (*R v Golder* (1960)), but that it may have a bearing on the credibility of the testimony of that witness in court (*R v Governor of Pentonville Prison ex p Alves* (1993)).

The manner in which a witness should be cross-examined about previous inconsistent statements is governed by provisions in the Criminal Procedure Act 1865, which applies to civil as well as to criminal proceedings.

Section 4 applies to both oral and written statements (*R v Derby Magistrates Court ex p B* (1996)) and is declaratory of the common law. It provides that if a witness who has made a previous inconsistent statement does not 'distinctly' admit that he has done so, proof may be given that he did make it. But before such proof can be given, the circumstances of the supposed statement, sufficient to designate the particular occasion, must be mentioned to the witness. The 'circumstances' include, for example, details of the time of the earlier statement, the place where it was made, and particulars of other persons present when it was made (*Angus v Smith* (1829); *Carpenter v Wall* (1840)).

Section 5 applies to written statements only. Its effect is that a witness may be asked whether he made a statement and be cross-examined about its general nature without being shown the document. But if the cross-examiner intends to use it as a contradictory statement, he must put it in evidence, and the witness must be given the opportunity to explain the contradiction.

## Re-examination

The object of re-examination is to clarify and complete any matters referred to in cross-examination and left in an ambiguous or incomplete state. It is not permitted to ask questions in re-examination unless they arise out of matters dealt with in cross-examination (*R v Fletcher* (1829)).

## Refreshing memory

A witness may refresh his memory from a note while giving evidence if it is a 'contemporaneous' one. It need not have been made literally contemporaneously, but must have been made as soon as possible after the events recorded, when they were still fresh in the witness' memory (*R v Richardson* (1971)). If the original note is not available, a transcript or later statement made from it may be used, provided it contains substantially what was in the note (*R v Cheng* (1976)).

'Refreshing memory' can refer to two different situations:

- where the witness' memory is actually jogged by the words on the page;

- where the events recorded were too long ago for the memory to be jogged, but the witness says he is sure the matters recorded are true (*Maugham v Hubbard* (1828)).

A witness may also refresh his memory outside court, before giving testimony, by re-reading his witness statement, even though that document was not made sufficiently contemporaneously to be used as a memory-refreshing document in the witness box (*R v Richardson* (1969)). It is desirable, though not essential, for the prosecution to tell the defence if their witnesses have done this (*R v Westwell* (1976)). A witness who has begun to give evidence but has difficulty in remembering may try to cure this by interrupting his evidence and reading his witness statement silently, whether or not he read that statement outside court before going into the witness box (*R v South Ribble Magistrates ex p Cochrane* (1996)). But he may not use the statement in the witness box as if it were a contemporaneous note.

Where a contemporaneous note is used as a memory-refreshing document, the following rules, laid down in *Senat v Senat* (1965), apply:

- cross-examining counsel may inspect the document. This alone will not make the document an exhibit;

- counsel may cross-examine on the document without making it an exhibit, provided the cross-examination does not go beyond the parts that were used to refresh the witness' memory;

- where cross-examination is on parts of the document not used to refresh the witness' memory, the document may be made an exhibit.

Where a memory-refreshing document becomes an exhibit in the case, the judge should direct the jury that it is not evidence of the truth of its contents, but only of the witness' credibility (*R v Virgo* (1978)).

### Previous consistent statements

There is a rule, sometimes referred to as 'the rule against narrative', that prohibits a witness from giving evidence that on some occasion before trial he made a statement that is consistent with his testimony at trial (*R v Roberts* (1942)).

Despite this rule, it is the practice to admit statements made by an accused person to the police, even if they contain, either wholly or in part, an exculpatory element.

*A wholly exculpatory statement*, though not evidence of the truth of its contents, is admissible to show the attitude of the defendant at the time he made it. This is not limited to statements made on first encounter with the police, though the longer the time that has elapsed since first encounter, the less weighty the evidence is likely to be. It is the duty of the prosecution to present the case fairly, and it would be unfair to give evidence of admissions (which are admissible under s 76 of the Police and Criminal Evidence Act 1984), but exclude answers favourable to the defendant (*R v Pearce* (1979)).

*A mixed statement* (containing some inculpatory and some exculpatory parts) is also admissible. The judge should tell the jury to consider the whole statement when determining where the truth lies, but he should usually point out that excuses are unlikely to have the same weight as incriminating parts (*R v Sharp* (1988)).

Previous consistent statements are also admissible in the following circumstances:

- to rebut an allegation of recent invention (*R v Oyesiku* (1971));

- where the statement was a 'recent complaint' in a sex case. To be admissible, the complaint must have been made as soon after the event alleged as could reasonably be expected; but this is liberally construed, and the personality of the complainant is taken into consideration in assessing reasonableness (*R v Valentine* (1996)). The mere fact that the statement was made in answer to a question does not make what was said inadmissible, provided the question was not of a leading nature (*R v Lillyman* (1986)). The judge in summing up should tell the jury that evidence of a complaint may possibly help them to decide whether the complainant is telling the truth, but that it cannot be independent confirmation of her evidence because it does not come from a source independent of her (*R v Islam* (1998));

- where the statement is part of the *res gestae* (see Chapter 7);

- as evidence of previous identification (see Chapter 9).

## Hostile witnesses

A witness who fails to give the evidence expected of him may do so for honest reasons. Such a witness is merely 'unfavourable', and the advocate who calls him will have no remedy but to call other witnesses to give a different account of events. But if the witness fails to say what is expected because he is not desirous of telling the truth to the court at the instance of the party calling him, he will be a 'hostile' witness. A witness ruled hostile by the judge may be cross-examined by the party calling him with a view to showing that he said something different on an earlier occasion (s 3 of the Criminal Procedure Act 1865; *R v Thompson* (1976)). But he may not be cross-examined with a view to discrediting him by showing that he is of bad character (*Wright v Beckett* (1834)).

## Collateral questions

A witness' answers to questions on 'collateral' (or ancillary) matters are said to be 'final', in the sense that evidence may not subsequently be adduced to rebut the answer given by the witness. But note the following exceptions:

- by s 6 of the Criminal Procedure Act 1865, a witness' previous convictions may be proved where he denies them or refuses to answer;

- if a witness denies that he is biased, either for or against a party, evidence may be called to disprove him (*R v Phillips* (1936));

- evidence may be given of a witness' general reputation for untruthfulness (*R v Richardson* (1968));

- evidence may be given of a physical or mental disability affecting a witness' reliability (*Toohey v Metropolitan Police Commissioner* (1965)).

# 4  Burden and standard of proof

## Burden of proof

The 'burden of proof' is the obligation which rests on a party in relation to a particular issue of fact in a civil or criminal case, and which must be 'discharged' or 'satisfied' if that party is to win on the issue in question. This burden is often referred to as the 'legal' or 'persuasive' burden, but must be distinguished from the *evidential burden* (see below).

### Burden of proof in civil cases

In the absence of relevant case law or statutory provision, resort must be had, in doubtful cases, to general guidelines. Note especially the dicta of Viscount Maugham in *Constantine (Joseph) SS Line Ltd v Imperial Smelting* (1942):

- the burden should lie on the party who affirms a proposition, rather than on the party who denies it (but the courts avoid a mechanical approach to the 'affirmation or denial' test: see *Soward v Leggatt* (1836));

- the burden of proof in any particular case depends on the circumstances under which the claim arises.

In other words, where the burden of proof should rest is merely a question of policy and fairness based on experience in the different situations (*Rustad v Great Northern Ry Co* (1913)). In looking at those situations a court will be concerned with, amongst other things, the ease with which a party may be able to discharge a burden of proof. See, for example, the following cases:

### The Glendarroch (1894)

In a contract for carriage of goods by sea, the shippers were exempt from liability for damage caused by perils of the sea, unless the damage was due to their own negligence. The goods were damaged when the ship became stranded.

*Held*: the owners of the goods had to prove the contract and non-delivery. The shippers had to show that the loss was caused by perils of the sea. It was then for the owners of the goods to establish the exception to that exception by proving that the shippers had been negligent.

### Hurst v Evans (1917)

The plaintiff insured his goods against loss or damage by any cause, with the exception of loss or damage caused by the theft or dishonesty of his own servants.

*Held*: the burden of proof was on the plaintiff, when he made a claim, to show that his loss did not come within the exceptions.

### Constantine (Joseph) SS Line Ltd v Imperial Smelting (1942)

Frustration was pleaded by shipowners as a defence to a claim by charterers.

*Held*: it was not necessary for the shipowners to prove that the frustrating event had occurred without fault on their part. The burden was on the charterers to prove negligence by the shipowners so as to bar them from relying on frustration.

### Levison v Patent Steam Carpet Cleaning Co (1978)

The defendant cleaners relied on an exclusion clause when goods sent to them for cleaning were lost. This clause would not assist them if they had been guilty of a fundamental breach of contract.

*Held*: it was for the cleaners to prove they had not been guilty of fundamental breach, and not for the customer to prove that they had.

**Burden of proof in criminal cases**

The basic rule was laid down by Viscount Sankey in *Woolmington v DPP* (1935):

> Throughout the web of English criminal law one golden thread is always to be seen, that it is the duty of the prosecution to prove the prisoner's guilt.

Viscount Sankey said that the rule was subject to exceptions in the case of the defence of insanity, and subject also to any statutory exception. There is no problem in seeing where the burdens lie if a statute provides, for example, that an accused person shall be guilty of an offence 'unless the contrary is proved' (s 2 of the Prevention of Corruption Act 1916). But the question whether Parliament in any given case has *impliedly* overruled *Woolmington* is more difficult to resolve.

By s 101 of the Magistrates' Courts Act 1980, where the defendant relies for his defence on any 'exception, exemption, proviso, excuse or qualification', whether or not it is part of the description of the offence, the burden of proving such a defence shall be on him. In *R v Edwards* (1975) the Court of Appeal held that this principle was not confined to cases heard in the magistrates' courts; the provision was a statutory statement of a common law rule applicable in all criminal courts.

In *R v Edwards* Lawton LJ spoke of the need, when applying this principle, to construe the statute on which the charge was based to determine where the burden of proof lay. This task of interpretation was subsequently emphasised by the

House of Lords in *R v Hunt* (1987), where it was held that the classification of defences for s 101 purposes was not constrained by the form of words used, or their position in the statute creating the offence. A more subtle approach to interpretation was required, which would pay regard to the wording of the Act, but would also take into account the mischief at which it was aimed, as well as practical matters affecting the burden of proof. Some guidelines were suggested by Lord Griffiths:

• courts should be very slow to classify a defence as falling within s 101, because Parliament can never lightly be taken to have intended to impose an onerous duty on a defendant to prove his innocence in a criminal case;

• the ease and difficulty likely to be encountered by the parties in discharging a legal burden are of great importance;

• the gravity of the offence must be considered.

But the task of interpretation is a difficult one, for at least four reasons:

(a) the question whether a given statutory provision falls within the class of 'any exception, exemption, proviso, excuse or qualification' is inherently problematic: see, for example, *Nimmo v Alexander Cowan and Sons Ltd* (1967);

(b) s 101 has been only haphazardly applied. Compare, for example, *Gatland v Metropolitan Police Commissioner* (1968) and *Nagy v Weston* (1965), and see offences under the Criminal Damage Act 1971;

(c) the project of distinguishing between rules and exceptions for s 101 purposes may be logically flawed because, rationally regarded, an exception is part of a rule;

(d) the reliance on policy that was authorised by *Nimmo v Alexander Cowan and Sons Ltd* (1967) and *R v Hunt* (1987) makes for uncertainty in interpretation.

## The evidential burden

This is not strictly a burden of proof at all. It is best seen as a rule of common sense, which says that there must be *some* evidence for a particular issue to become a live one, so as to be fit for consideration by the jury or some other tribunal of fact. Whether an evidential burden has been satisfied is a matter solely for the judge.

In a criminal trial, the defence will have an evidential burden in relation to any issue that the prosecution are not required to raise. One obvious example is where the defence have a legal burden to satisfy in relation to any issue. But although the defence do not, except for the defence of insanity, have a legal burden to establish common law defences, they may still have an evidential burden, for example, where the defence raised is that of self-defence (*R v Lobell* (1957)), duress (*R v Gill* (1963)), non-insane automatism (*Bratty v AG for Northern Ireland* (1963)), and provocation (*Mancini v DPP* (1942)). NB: the absence of consent in rape is an essential element of the offence, in respect of which the prosecution have both a legal and an evidential burden (*Selvey v DPP* (1970)).

## Standard of proof

### The criminal standard

Two formulas are traditional. Jurors may be told, 'You must be satisfied so that you are sure', or 'You must be satisfied beyond reasonable doubt' of the defendant's guilt. But it is the effect of the summing-up as a whole that matters, and the formulas do not have to be exactly followed provided their gist is explained to the jury (*Walters v The Queen* (1969)).

Where there is a legal burden on the defendant to prove something in a criminal case, proof is required only to the civil standard (*R v Carr-Briant* (1943)).

### The civil standard

A lower standard of proof is required in civil cases: proof on the balance of probabilities (*Miller v Minister of Pensions* (1947)). Where a serious allegation is made, for example, of conduct amounting to a criminal offence, proof is still only to the civil standard. But the inherent improbability of such an allegation is taken into account when deciding whether the evidence is of sufficient weight to satisfy the court that the allegation has been proved. Earlier suggestions that a third standard existed, at some point between the ordinary civil standard and the criminal standard, were discredited in *Re H* (1996) by the House of Lords.

# 5 Presumptions

There are three types of presumption:

(a) presumptions of fact;

(b) irrebuttable presumptions of law;

(c) rebuttable presumptions of law.

## Presumptions of fact

A 'presumption of fact' is no more than an inference from facts that is part of the ordinary reasoning process. For example, by s 8 of the Criminal Justice Act 1967 there is a presumption of fact that people intend the natural consequences of their acts. The section provides that a court or jury, in determining whether a person has committed an offence, shall not be *bound in law* to infer that he intended the result of his actions by reason of its being a natural and probable consequence of those actions, but shall decide whether he did intend that result *by drawing inferences from all the evidence.*

## Irrebuttable presumptions of law

These are just the same as rules or principles of substantive law. For example, 'the presumption of innocence' is a way of referring to the principle that the burden of proof generally rests on the prosecution in a criminal case.

## Rebuttable presumptions of law

The general pattern of these presumptions is that once a party has proved certain basic facts, other facts will be presumed to exist in the absence of some evidence to the contrary. The amount of contrary evidence required depends on the substantive law applying to the particular situation.

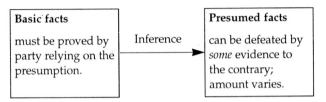

**Figure 5.1**

### Presumption of marriage

Where a man and a woman have gone through a ceremony of marriage followed by cohabitation, there is a presumption that the ceremony was valid. It was formerly held that the presumption could be rebutted only by evidence that went beyond a mere balance of probability (*Piers v Piers* (1849)), but the modern view of standards of proof suggests that rebuttal on the balance of probabilities would suffice (*Re H* (1996)).

Even where there is no evidence that a ceremony of marriage has been performed, a presumption that a man and woman were lawfully married will arise from evidence of cohabitation, coupled with their reputation as man and wife (*In re Taylor, decd* (1961)).

### Presumption of legitimacy

There is a presumption that a child born or conceived during wedlock is the child of the woman's husband. The presumption applies not only where the husband and wife are living together, but also where they are living apart, whether by a formal or informal agreement. The presumption does not apply where the parties are separated by a court order. But it will apply after the presentation of a petition for divorce or nullity, and even after the grant of a decree nisi (as opposed to a decree absolute) of divorce or nullity (*Knowles v Knowles* (1962)).

By s 26 of the Family Law Reform Act 1969, the presumption may be rebutted by evidence which shows that it is more probable than not that the person in question is legitimate or illegitimate, as the case may be.

### Presumption of death
Some statutory provisions require a court to presume the death of a person in certain circumstances. There is also a common law presumption of death, as follows:

> Where as regards a certain person there is no acceptable evidence that he was alive at some time during a continuous period of seven years or more, then he will be presumed to have died at some time during that period if it can be proved that:

- there are persons who would be likely to have heard of him during that period;

- those persons have not heard of him; and,

- all due inquiries have been made appropriate to the circumstances.

See *Chard v Chard* (1956).

### Res ipsa loquitur
This maxim, meaning 'the thing speaks for itself', was traditionally regarded as giving rise to some kind of presumption in actions for negligence. Where something

**EVIDENCE**

which had caused an accident was shown to have been under the management of the defendant or his servants, and the accident was such as in the ordinary course of things did not happen if those who had management used proper care, the accident itself led to an inference of negligence (*Moore v R Fox & Sons* (1956)).

More recently, the maxim has been described as 'no more than an exotic, although convenient, phrase' to describe a common sense approach to the assessment of evidence. It means that a plaintiff *prima facie* establishes negligence where:

• it is not possible for him to prove precisely what was the relevant act or omission that set in train the events leading to the accident; but

• on the evidence as it stands at the close of the plaintiff's case it is more likely than not that the cause of the accident was some act or omission of the defendant, or of someone for whom the defendant is responsible, involving failure to take proper care for the plaintiff's safety.

It is misleading to talk of the burden of proof 'shifting' in a case where *res ipsa loquitur* applies. In any action for negligence the burden of proof rests throughout on the plaintiff. In an appropriate case the plaintiff will establish a *prima facie* case by relying on the fact of the accident. If the defendant adduces no evidence, there will be nothing to rebut the inference of negligence and the plaintiff's case will have been proved. But if the defendant does adduce evidence, it must be evaluated to see if it is still reasonable to draw the inference of negligence from the mere fact of the accident (*Ng Chun Pui v Lee Chuen Tat* (1988)).

**Presumption of regularity**

This expression can refer to two different presumptions:

(a) the presumption that official appointments have been properly and formally made, and that official acts have been properly and formally performed, for example, *R v Verelst* (1813), where the defendant was charged with committing perjury while giving evidence in an ecclesiastical court, and it was held that the prosecution did not have to prove that the court official who administered the oath had been properly appointed. It was held in *Dillon v The Queen* (1982) that the presumption could not be relied on in a criminal trial to establish a central element of the offence charged. It is unclear whether the presumption, where it does apply, places a legal or merely an evidential burden on the person against whom it is to be used;

(b) the presumption that a mechanical instrument, provided it is of a kind that is usually in working order, was in working order at a particular time that is relevant in the litigation. The effect of the presumption is to place an evidential burden only on the person against whom it is to be used. The presumption has been said to apply to watches and speedometers (*Nicholas v Penney* (1950)), and to traffic lights (*Tingle Jacobs & Co v Kennedy* (1964)). In relation to computers, it is clear that in criminal cases the presumption does not apply (s 69 of PACE 1984); the question appears not to have arisen in a civil case.

# 6 Hearsay: scope

## Statement of the rule

An assertion other than one made by a person while giving oral evidence in the proceedings is inadmissible as evidence of any fact asserted. [*R v Sharp* (1988), *per* Lord Havers LC.]

'Assertion' includes assertions of opinion.

The assertion may have been made orally, in writing, or in some other way (*Chandrasekera v R* (1937)).

The rule covers:

- previous out of court assertions made by persons who give evidence in the proceedings;

- out of court assertions made by persons who do not give evidence in the proceedings.

In *Myers v DPP* (1965) the House of Lords said that it was not permissible for judges to create new common law exceptions to the hearsay rule, but the courts have in some cases ignored a hearsay problem. This is clear, for example, from the rules that have developed allowing witnesses to 'refresh their memories' when giving evidence (*Maugham v Hubbard* (1828)); from the evidential status of 'mixed' statements made by accused persons to the police (*R v Sharp* (1988)); from the rules relating to expert opinion evidence (*R v Abadom* (1983)); and from the rules about evidence of previous identification (*R v Osbourne and Virtue* (1973)).

What was said out of court must have been an assertion, that is, a piece of narrative or description. Thus in *Sparks v R* (1964) the defendant was not allowed to adduce evidence of a child's statement to her mother that it was 'a coloured boy' who had assaulted her. But in *Woodhouse v Hall* (1980), where the defendant was charged with acting in the management of a brothel, it was held that a police officer should have been allowed to give evidence that he had been offered sexual services at a massage parlour managed by the defendant. The reason for this was that the offer amounted in law to more than a mere assertion; it was a verbal act with legal consequences, because it brought the premises within the common law definition of a brothel.

An assertion may be either express or implied. There is no legal definition of an implied assertion, but the expression appears to cover a situation where:

- a speaker makes a non-assertive out of court utterance (or, possibly, performs an action);

- he would not have made that utterance (or performed the action) if he had not believed a particular state of affairs to exist;

- evidence of the out of court non-assertive utterance (or action) is adduced to prove that (a) he did have that belief, and therefore that (b) the state of affairs at the time corresponded to his belief.

Thus, in *R v Kearley* (1992), it was held that the prosecution could not adduce evidence, in order to prove the defendant's possession of drugs with intent to supply, of telephone calls and visits to the defendant's premises, made by persons inquiring about the purchase of drugs. And in *Wright v Doe d Tatham* (1837) Parke B said, obiter, that in order to establish the seaworthiness of a ship it would be impermissible to give evidence of the fact that, before the ship sailed, the captain had examined it carefully and had then gone on board with his family.

The evidence must be adduced to prove the truth of what has been expressly or impliedly asserted. Thus, the hearsay rule does not apply where the fact of the assertion is relevant for some reason other than the truth of the facts asserted, for example, where the evidence is adduced:

- to show that what was asserted was false, rather than true (*Mawaz Khan v The Queen* (1967);

- to show that someone to whom the assertion was made might have acted under duress (*Subramaniam v Public Prosecutor* (1956));

- to show that the defendant had an interest in the matters asserted (*R v Lydon* (1987); *R v McIntosh* (1992)).

**Is an utterance (or action) caught, in principle, by the rule against hearsay?**

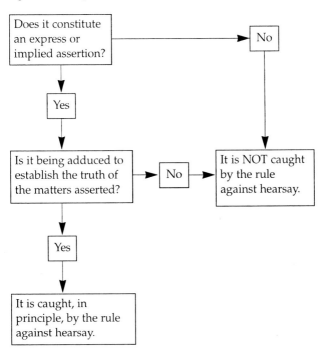

**Figure 6.1**

## Evidence produced by machines

The hearsay rule does not exclude tapes, films or still photographs that have directly recorded an incident as it took place (*R v Dodson* (1984); *Taylor v Chief Constable of Cheshire* (1987)).

The hearsay rule does not apply to documents produced by machines that automatically record some process or event, such as a print-out from a computer recording telephone calls from a given number (*R v Spiby* (1990)), or from an Intoximeter recording the level of alcohol in breath (*Castle v Cross* (1984)). Nor does the rule apply to readings from a machine that simply carries out arithmetical procedures (*R v Wood* (1982)).

But the hearsay rule will apply where there has been some human intervention in the recording process, for example, where an employee has previously compiled records and someone else has transferred them to a computer (*R v Coventry JJ ex p Bullard* (1992)).

## Negative hearsay

An inference may be drawn from the non-existence of a document, or entry in a document, without offending the rule against hearsay. A witness with personal knowledge of the compilation and custody of the relevant records must be called to give evidence of the absence of the document or entry, and its significance (*R v Patel* (1981); *R v Shone* (1983)).

# 7 Hearsay: common law exceptions

The common law developed a number of exceptions to the hearsay rule, several of which are now virtually obsolete. Since the Civil Evidence Act 1995 abolished the hearsay rule in civil proceedings, the common law exceptions are now of significance only in criminal cases. The main exceptions are:

- certain statements by deceased persons;

- statements admitted as 'part of the *res gestae*';

- statements made in furtherance of a common purpose.

## Statements by deceased persons

There is no general exception at common law for the admissibility of statements by persons who have died since making them. To be admissible, the statement must fall into one of several categories developed by the courts. Of these, only two are likely to be of significance:

### Declarations against pecuniary or proprietary interest

In *R v Rogers* (1995), the Court of Appeal laid down four conditions for admissibility:

(a) the deceased must have had a 'peculiar' (that is, particular or special) means of knowing the facts stated;

(b) the interest against which the declaration was made must be either proprietary or pecuniary; a mere declaration against penal interest will not suffice. But the pecuniary or proprietary interest does not have to be recognised by the law, or even by morality;

(c) the declaration must be against the interest of the deceased at the time when it was made; that is, it must refer to a present obligation, and not to one arising in the future;

(d) the declarant must know that the declaration is against his interest at the time when he makes it.

A declaration against pecuniary or proprietary interest may be adduced to prove not only the truth of its contents, but the truth of other facts connected to it. But this will be the case only where the connected facts are necessary to explain the nature of the declaration. Compare, for example, *Higham v Ridgway* (1808) and *R v Rogers* (1995);

### Dying declarations in cases of murder or manslaughter

A declaration as to the circumstances of his death made by a declarant under a settled, hopeless expectation of imminent death is admissible to prove the cause of death (*Mills v R* (1995)). It is unclear whether a dying declaration would be admissible in a prosecution for causing death by dangerous driving. The declarant must be someone who would have been competent as a witness, had he survived (*R v Pike* (1829)).

There must be no hope of recovery at the time when the declaration is made (*R v Jenkins* (1869)). But so long as the state of mind was the correct one when the declaration was made, it does not matter if the victim developed hopes of recovery afterwards (*R v Austin* (1912)). That death did not in fact occur for some time is irrelevant (*R v Bernadotti* (1869)).

A dying declaration that helps the defence is also admissible (*R v Scaife* (1836)). If the conditions for this exception cannot be proved, it may be possible to use the *res gestae* exception (see below).

## Res gestae statements

The Latin expression '*res gestae*' may be loosely translated as 'events occurring' or 'things happening'. If a statement is said to be part of the *res gestae*, what is meant is that it is an out of court statement so closely associated with the circumstances in which it was made as to guarantee a greater reliability than usual. The courts have distinguished four different situations.

### Excited utterances

These are the spontaneous exclamations of the victim of an offence or of an observer. Although most of the cases are about victims' utterances, this exception is not confined to them (*Milne v Leisler* (1862)). In *R v Andrews* (1987) the test for admissibility under this exception was laid down as follows:

(a) the primary question that the judge must ask is whether the possibility of concoction or distortion by the original speaker can be disregarded;

(b) to answer that question, the judge must first consider the circumstances in which the particular statement was made, in order to satisfy himself that the event was so unusual, startling or dramatic as to dominate the thoughts of the speaker to the extent that his utterance was an instinctive reaction to that event, giving no time for reasoned reflection. In such a situation, the judge would be entitled to conclude that the involvement or pressure of the event excluded the possibility of concoction or distortion, provided the statement was made in conditions of approximate contemporaneity;

(c) for the statement to be sufficiently spontaneous it must be so closely associated with the startling event that the mind of the speaker was still dominated by that event. The fact that a statement was made in answer to a question is only something to be taken into consideration under this head; it does not mean that the statement will inevitably lack sufficient spontaneity;

(d) quite apart from the time factor, there may be special features in the case that relate to the possibility of concoction or distortion by the original speaker, for example, a motive for fabrication. Where a feature of this kind exists, the judge must be satisfied that there was no possibility of any concoction or distortion to the advantage of the speaker or the disadvantage of the defendant;

(e) the ordinary fallibility of human recollection may affect the *weight* of the testifying witness' evidence, but is not relevant to the question of *admissibility*. However, there may be special features giving rise to the possibility of error, for example, where the original speaker was drunk, or had made an identification in particularly difficult circumstances. If there are special features such as these, the judge must consider whether he can still exclude the possibility of error before admitting the evidence;

(f) where the trial judge has properly directed himself as to the correct approach to the evidence, and there is material that entitles him to reach his conclusions, the Court of Appeal will not interfere with his decision.

---

**An *Andrews* check list**

- Was the nature of the event such as to make what was said an instinctive reaction to it?

- How close in time were the words to the event?

- Were there any special features to suggest that the original speaker might have given a *dishonest* account of the event?

- Were there any special features, apart from the fallibility of ordinary memory, to suggest that the original speaker might have given a *mistaken* account of the event?

---

**Figure 7.1**

The nature of the event itself and the lapse of time between the event and the statement, are likely to feature in arguments about admissibility. The less dramatic the event, and the greater the lapse of time, the less likely it will be that the speaker's mind was still dominated by the event, so as to rule out any opportunity for concoction or distortion. Compare *Tobi v Nicholas* (1987) and *R v Carnall* (1995).

**Statements relating to the speaker's contemporaneous state of mind or emotion**
An obvious example is a defendant's expression of antipathy towards a murder victim shortly before the latter's death (see Lord Atkinson during argument in *R v Ball* (1911)).

An expression of intention to do something has sometimes been relied on to prove that the speaker carried out the act in question. See *R v Buckley* (1873); *R v Moghal* (1977); but cf *R v Wainwright* (1875); *R v Thomson* (1912).

### Statements relating to the maker's contemporaneous physical sensations

The usefulness of this exception is limited, because while such statements are admissible as evidence of the sensations, they are inadmissible to prove their cause (*R v Gloster* (1888)). It is possible that 'contemporaneous' may be flexibly interpreted: see *R v Black* (1922).

### Statements relating to the maker's performance of an act

A statement that is made at the time of performing a relevant act is admissible to explain the act, provided it is made roughly contemporaneously by the person who performs the act (*Howe v Malkin* (1878)).

## Statements in furtherance of a common purpose

Where defendants are charged with conspiracy, or charged jointly with an offence where the prosecution allege a common enterprise, evidence of acts done or statements made by one defendant in furtherance of the common enterprise will be admissible against other defendants, even though those other defendants were not present at the time when the act was done or statement made. The reason for this is that a combination of persons for the purpose of committing a crime is regarded as implying an authority in each to act or speak in furtherance of the common purpose on behalf of the others (*R v Gray* (1995)).

There must be independent evidence to prove that the defendant, against whom another's act or statement is to be used, was a member of the common enterprise (*R v Governor of Pentonville Prison ex p Osman* (1990)).

Where what was said by one defendant amounted to no more than a narrative, it will be capable of being used against other defendants only if it was said in furtherance of the common enterprise. This would rule out a confession to the police, but might well include a briefing during the course of the enterprise: see *R v Jones* (1997).

# 8 Hearsay: statutory exceptions

## Documentary hearsay under the Criminal Justice Act 1988

Sections 23 and 24 of the Criminal Justice Act 1988 allow for the admissibility of written hearsay in certain cases. Both sections must be read in the light of either s 25 or s 26.

Sections 23 and 24 are both confined to 'a statement made by a person in a document'. 'Statement' means any representation of fact, however made, and 'document' means anything in which information of any description is recorded (Sched 2, para 5(1) of the Criminal Justice Act 1988, as amended by Sched 1, para 12 of the Civil Evidence Act 1995). Whether the statement has been 'made' by the relevant person may be a matter for argument. In *R v McGillivray* (1993) the victim of a crime was unable because of physical disability to sign a police officer's record of his oral account of events, but he orally agreed to the accuracy of the record when the officer read it back to him. It was held that the written statement had been made by the victim.

Where evidence has been given by witness statement, it is not enough for the judge in summing up simply to draw the jury's attention to that fact. He must specifically:

- remind the jury that the maker of the statement has not been in court to be cross-examined;

- tell the jury that because of this, they should take particular care with that evidence.

See *R v Curry* (1998).

**Section 23 of the Criminal Justice Act 1988**

The section provides that, subject to certain conditions, a statement made by a person in a document shall be admissible in criminal proceedings as evidence of any fact of which direct oral evidence by him would be admissible. The section is therefore normally confined to first hand documentary hearsay. If the document contains hearsay that falls within a common law exception to the rule, it is likely that that hearsay element will be admissible under s 23: see *The Ymnos* (1981); *R v Lockley* (1995); *R v James* (1996); for a contrary argument, see Law Com No 245 (1997), paras 8.25–8.26.

Section 23 applies only where the person who made the statement (M) is unavailable for a reason set out in sub-ss (2) or (3).

The conditions in sub-s (2) are that:

(a) M is dead, or unfit to attend as a witness by reason of his bodily or mental condition; *or*

(b) M is outside the UK, and it is not reasonably practicable to secure his attendance; *or*

(c) all reasonable steps have been taken to find M, but he cannot be found.

The condition in sub-s (3) is that:

(a) the statement was made to a police officer or some other person charged with the duty of investigating offences or charging offenders; *and*

(b) the person who made the statement does not give oral evidence through fear, or because he is kept out of the way.

## Not reasonably practicable to secure attendance

In *R v Castillo* (1996) the Court of Appeal held that the mere fact that it is possible for a witness to attend does not mean that his attendance is reasonably practicable. To determine this question the judge has to consider several factors, including:

- the importance of the evidence and the extent to which the witness' non-attendance is prejudicial to the defence;

- the expense and inconvenience of securing the witness' attendance; and

- the reasons why it is not convenient or reasonably practicable for the witness to attend.

## Does not give evidence through fear

The fear does not have to be based on reasonable grounds (*R v Acton JJ ex p McMullen* (1990)). Although it will be *sufficient* that the witness' fear is a consequence of the commission of the offence, or of something said or done subsequently in relation to that offence, it is not *necessary* that the fear should arise in either of these ways. Provided fear is established, there is no need for the court to inquire into the basis of it (*R v Martin* (1996)).

Sub-section 23(3)(b) can be relied on even though the witness has already begun to give evidence (*R v Waters* (1997)).

In *R v Belmarsh Magistrates' Court ex p Gilligan* (1998) the Divisional Court held that in order to satisfy the requirements of s 23, it is necessary for the court to hear oral evidence as to the existence of fear, for example, from a police officer who has recently spoken to the witness. In that case a second written statement from the witness asserting his fear was held to be insufficient to justify the admission of an earlier written statement, in which the witness had provided evidence against the defendant.

The relevant condition must be proved under s 23 by evidence that is itself admissible, without any reliance on the statute (*R v Case* (1991)).

---

**Checklist for availability of s 23**

- Was the statement made by a person in a document?

- Could the maker of the written statement have given oral evidence of the matters to which it relates?

- Is the maker of the statement unavailable for one of the reasons set out in sub-ss (2) or (3)?

- Can the reason be proved without relying on the statute?

If the answer to each of the above is 'Yes', s 23 will be available, subject to s 25 or s 26.

---

**Section 24 of the Criminal Justice Act 1988**
This section makes admissible in certain circumstances documents created or received by a person in the course of a trade, business, profession or other occupation, or as the holder of a paid or unpaid office. Section 24 statements may include multiple hearsay provided:

- each person supplying the information had, or may reasonably be supposed to have had, personal knowledge of the matters dealt with (s 24(1)(ii)); and

- each person supplying the information received it in the course of a trade, business, profession or other occupation, or as the holder of a paid or unpaid office (s 24(2)).

By s 24(4), a document prepared for the purposes of pending or contemplated criminal proceedings or a criminal investigation shall be inadmissible under s 24(1) unless one of the requirements in s 23(2) is satisfied, or the requirements of s 23(3) are satisfied, or the person who made the statement cannot reasonably be expected to have any recollection of the matters dealt with in the statement.

In s 24(1)(ii) a distinction is drawn between the maker of a statement and a supplier of information. In *Brown v Secretary of State for Social Security* (1994), the Divisional Court held that where the person who supplied the information contained in the document is not the same as the person who brought the document into existence, the maker of the statement (the person who must be unavailable or unable to remember) is the person who brought the document into existence; it is not the person who supplied the information contained in the document. See also *R v Bedi* (1992); *R v Field* (1992).

While under s 23 the existence of the appropriate conditions of admissibility must be proved by independently admissible evidence (*R v Case* (1991)), the existence of the s 24(1) conditions can be inferred from the document under consideration (*R v Foxley* (1995); *R v Ilyas* (1996)).

**Checklist for availability of s 24**

- Was the document created or received by a person in the course of a trade, etc?

- Can this be proved at least by inference from the document?

- If the information passed through more than one person before being recorded:

  o did each person have, or may he reasonably be supposed to have had, personal knowledge of the matters dealt with; *and*

  o did each person supplying the information receive it in the course of a trade, etc?

- If the document was prepared for the purposes of pending or contemplated criminal proceedings or a criminal investigation:

  o is one of the s 23(2) requirements satisfied; *or*

  o are the requirements of s 23(3) satisfied; *or*

  o is it the case that the person who made the statement (who may not be the same as the person supplying the information) cannot reasonably be expected to have any recollection of the matters dealt with in the statement?

If the answer to each of the above is 'Yes', then s 24 will be available, subject to s 25 or s 26.

## Sections 25 and 26 of the Criminal Justice Act 1988

By s 25, if, having regard to all the circumstances, the court is of the opinion that a statement admissible under s 23 or s 24 'in the interests of justice ought not to be admitted', it may direct that it be not admitted. Thus, if s 25 applies, there is a presumption in favour of admitting the evidence (*R v Cole* (1990)). In considering admissibility, the court must have regard to the matters set out in s 25(2), which include:

- the nature, source and likely authenticity of the document containing the statement;

- the extent to which the statement appears to supply evidence that would otherwise not be readily available;

- the relevance of the evidence;

- any risk of unfairness to a defendant, having regard in particular to whether it is likely to be possible to controvert the statement if the person making it does not attend to give oral evidence.

By contrast, under s 26, which deals with documents prepared for the purpose of criminal proceedings or investigations, a statement admissible in principle under s 23 or s 24 *shall not* be given in evidence, unless the court is of the opinion that the statement 'ought to be admitted in the interests of justice'. Here, the presumption is in favour of exclusion. The court is not to admit the statement unless made to hold the opinion that in the interests of justice it ought to be admitted (*R v Cole* (1990)). In considering admissibility, the court must have regard to:

- the contents of the statement;

- any risk of unfairness to a defendant, having regard in particular to whether it is likely to be possible to controvert the statement if the person making it does not attend to give oral evidence;

- any other relevant circumstances.

When considering under ss 25 or 26 whether it will be possible for a defendant to controvert the evidence of the statement maker, the court takes into account various opportunities for this. They include, in addition to the defendant's own testimony:

- cross-examination of other prosecution witnesses;

- calling other defence witnesses;

- putting the credibility of the statement maker in issue under Sched 2 of the Act.

See *R v Cole* (1990); *R v Gokal* (1997).

Where documentary hearsay is admitted under ss 23 or 24, Sched 2 of the Act makes admissible any evidence which, if *the person making the statement* had been called as a witness, would have been admissible as relevant to his credibility, for example, evidence of previous convictions. If the court gives leave, evidence may be given of any matters relevant to credibility about which that person could have been cross-examined, even though they would have been collateral matters on which his answer would have been final. Evidence may also be given of any contradictory statements made by that person, either before or after he made the statement admitted as documentary hearsay. But if reliance has been placed on s 24, this may be of little help to a defendant, because it may be the credibility of *the supplier of information*, rather than the credibility of the maker of the document, that the defendant will wish to challenge.

The existence of a discretion means that cases are decided very much on their own facts, but it has been said that the crucial factor for determining the exercise of the discretion is the quality of the evidence (*R v Cole* (1990)). If the quality of the evidence is good enough, a documentary statement may be admitted even where it forms the main evidence against the defendant (*R v Dragic* (1996)).

## Video recordings of children's evidence

The relevant provision is s 32A of the Criminal Justice Act 1988 (created by the Criminal Justice Act 1991, s 54, and amended by the Criminal Justice and Public Order Act 1994, s 50). The section makes admissible, in certain circumstances, subject to the leave of the court, a video recording of an interview with a child. The object is that the video recording shall take the place of examination-in-chief, although the child must be available for cross-examination.

The section applies to trials on indictment and in youth courts, and to appeals from such proceedings, for offences in two categories:

- those involving assault on, or injury or threat of injury to, a person, or offences under s 1 of the Children and Young Persons Act 1933 (cruelty to persons under 16);

- various statutory sexual offences or offences involving indecency.

By s 32A(3) the court shall give leave for a video recording to be tendered in evidence unless:

- it appears that the child will not be available for cross-examination; or

- the court is of the opinion that in the interests of justice the recording ought not to be admitted.

Where the proceedings are in relation to an offence in the first of the categories referred to, a 'child' means a person under 14 when the recording was made. Where the proceedings are in relation to an offence in the second category, 'child' means a person under 17 when the recording was made.

### The Civil Evidence Act 1995

By s 1(1) of the Act, in civil proceedings evidence shall not be excluded on the ground that it is hearsay. Multiple as well as first hand hearsay is admissible.

Sections 2 to 4 provide safeguards in relation to hearsay evidence. There is a general duty on parties under s 2(1) to give warning of the intention to adduce hearsay evidence. But by s 2(4) failure to comply with this duty is not to affect the admissibility of the evidence. Section 3 provides a power to call for cross-examination a person whose statement has been tendered as hearsay evidence. Statutory guidelines for weighing hearsay evidence are provided in s 4.

Sections 5 to 7 are supplementary provisions. The maker of a statement adduced as hearsay evidence must have been competent to give direct oral evidence at the time the statement was made. There are provisions to admit evidence to attack or support the credibility of the maker of a hearsay statement, as well as evidence to show that the maker of the statement made inconsistent statements, either before or after the statement was made.

By s 8, where a statement contained in a document is admissible as evidence in civil proceedings, it can be proved by the production of the original document or a copy authenticated in such manner as the court shall approve. It is immaterial how many removes there are between a copy and the original.

Section 9 concerns the proof of records of a business or public authority. Its effect is that documents, including those stored by a computer, forming part of such records are admissible as hearsay evidence under s 1, and the ordinary notice provisions apply. Unless the court otherwise directs, a document shall be taken to form part of the records of a business or public authority if there is produced to the court a certificate to that effect signed by an officer of the business or authority. The absence of an entry in such records may be proved by affidavit of an officer of the business or authority in question.

# 9 Hazardous evidence

Judges in the past attempted to control the way in which juries thought about kinds of evidence that were regarded as particularly unreliable. Early informal rules of practice later developed into formal rules of law about directions that should be given during a summing-up. One of these sets of rules came to be known as the law relating to 'corroboration', which required juries to be warned about the danger of convicting on the 'uncorroborated' evidence of a witness in three types of case: where the witness was an accomplice, a child, or a complainant in a case where a sexual crime was alleged. The law of corroboration has now been very largely abolished by s 34(2) of the Criminal Justice Act 1988 (in relation to the evidence of children), and s 32 of the Criminal Justice and Public Order Act 1994 (in relation to evidence of accomplices and of complainants in sexual cases). The effect of these sections was stated by the Court of Appeal in *R v Makanjuola* (1995) to be that trial judges now have a wide discretion to adapt warnings about the testimony of any witness to the circumstances of the case. But for a warning to be given, there must be some *evidential* basis for suggesting that the witness' testimony may be unreliable.

Despite the existence of this modern discretion, a body of case law has developed concerning warnings that a judge may be *bound* to give to the jury where lies have been told by a defendant. There also remains a body of case law about warnings concerning identification evidence, which has been unaffected by statute.

## Evidence of a defendant's lies

Evidence of lies told by a defendant inside or outside court can have probative value, but will often require a direction from the judge to ensure that the jury approaches such evidence with care. The direction is sometimes still called a *Lucas* direction after a case in 1981 in which the problem was discussed in the context of the old corroboration law.

The law on the subject was stated more recently in *R v Burge* (1996). According to this decision, the direction should contain two points:

(a) the lie must be admitted by the defendant, or the jury must find it proved beyond reasonable doubt, before the jury can take it into account;

(b) the jury must be warned that the mere fact that the defendant has lied is not in itself evidence of guilt, because defendants may lie for innocent reasons. Only if the jury is sure that the defendant did not lie for an innocent reason can a lie support the prosecution case. The effect of this is that the prosecution have to negative any innocent explanation for the defendant's lie before the jury can take it into account in deciding whether the case is proved.

According to *R v Burge*, a direction on these lines is usually required in four situations:

(a) where the defendant relies on an alibi;

(b) where the judge suggests that the jury look for something to support a possibly unreliable item of prosecution evidence, and points to an alleged lie by the defendant as potential support;

(c) where the prosecution try to show that the defendant has told a lie, either in or out of court, about a matter apart from the offence charged, but which points to the guilt of the defendant on that charge;

(d) where the jury might adopt such an argument, even though the prosecution has not used it.

But a *Burge* direction is not required in every case where a defendant testifies, merely because the jury might conclude that he told a lie about something while on oath. A direction will not be required where rejection by the jury of something the defendant said will leave them no choice but to convict. This will be the case where the prosecution evidence is in direct and irreconcilable conflict with the defendant's evidence on a matter central to the case (*R v Harron* (1996)), and may thus include in some cases, despite what was said in *R v Burge*, a lie about an alibi.

## Identification and *Turnbull* guidelines

In *R v Turnbull* (1977) the Court of Appeal laid down guidelines for judges summing up in cases where the prosecution rely on contested identification evidence. Failure to follow the guidelines is likely to lead to the quashing of a conviction as unsafe.

### When do the guidelines apply?
They apply whenever the prosecution case depends 'wholly or substantially' on the correctness of one or more identifications of the defendant, and the defence allege that the identifying witnesses are mistaken. A *Turnbull* direction must be given in cases where identification is based on recognition, as well as in other situations where there is a more obvious risk of error (*Shand v The Queen* (1996)).

The need for a *Turnbull* direction generally arises where the issue is whether the defendant was present at a particular place or not. Where his presence at the scene is not disputed, but his participation in the offence is, the direction does not have to be given automatically. It will be necessary to give it where there is the possibility that the witness has mistaken one person for another: for example, because of similarities of clothing, colour or build (*R v Slater* (1995)), or because of confused action (*R v Thornton* (1995)).

Where the defence is that an identifying witnesses is lying, rather than honestly mistaken, the cases in which a *Turnbull* warning can be wholly omitted will still be exceptional. (But for an example, see *R v Cape* (1996).) The judge should normally tell the jury to consider whether they are satisfied that the witness was not mistaken. But in such a case it will be enough to give the warning more briefly than in other cases (*Shand v The Queen* (1996)).

**What does a *Turnbull* direction require?**

A judge giving a *Turnbull* direction must do three things:

(a) warn the jury of the special need for caution before convicting the defendant on the evidence of identification;

(b) tell the jury the reason why such a warning is needed. Some reference should be made to the fact that a mistaken witness can be a convincing one, and that a number of such witnesses can all be mistaken. *R v Pattinson* (1996) suggests that there should be a reference to the risk of miscarriages of justice resulting from mistaken identifications;

(c) tell the jury to examine closely the circumstances in which each identification came to be made. But it is not necessary in every case for the judge to summarise for the jury all the weaknesses of the identification evidence. If he does choose to summarise that evidence, he should point to strengths as well as weaknesses (*R v Pattinson* (1996)).

Having warned the jury in accordance with the *Turnbull* direction, as developed in later cases, the judge should go on to direct the jury to consider whether the identification evidence is supported by any other evidence, identifying for them the evidence that is capable of providing such support.

It was said in *R v Turnbull* (1977) that where the quality of the identification evidence is good, the jury can safely be left to assess it without any supporting evidence, subject to an adequate warning. But where the quality is poor, the judge should withdraw the case from the jury at the end of the prosecution case unless there is other evidence to support the correctness of the identification.

## Identifications inside and outside court

### Dock identifications
It has been said that identification of a defendant for the first time when he is in the dock at trial is to be avoided (*R v Cartwright* (1914)). But in *Barnes v Chief Constable of Durham* (1997) the Divisional Court acknowledged that such evidence was acceptable in magistrates' courts in certain cases.

### Evidence of previous identifications
The evidence of a previous out of court identification of the defendant can be given by the person who made the identification, because it shows that the witness was able to identify the defendant at a time nearer to the events under

investigation, so reducing the chance of mistake (*R v Christie* (1914)).

The rule against hearsay has been relaxed to allow evidence to be given by an observer of someone else's out of court identification, even where the witness who made the original identification has failed to remember in court that she identified anybody (*R v Osbourne and Virtue* (1973)).

Neither the hearsay rule nor the rule against previous consistent statements applies to sketches (whether made by the witness himself or by a police artist on the basis of instructions from the witness), or to photofit pictures of a suspect (*R v Cook* (1987)).

### Voice identifications

There is little authority on this subject. *R v Hersey* (1998) shows that a 'voice identification parade' can be held. In that case the Court of Appeal said that where there has been a voice identification, the judge when summing up must tell the jury of the risk of mistaken identification on lines similar to those adopted in cases of visual identification.

## Code D of PACE 1984

Breaches of this code, which governs identification procedures, are likely to result in the exclusion of evidence because if the code is not followed, the reliability of the identification evidence is likely to be diminished.

There may sometimes be room for argument about whether Code D applies. In particular, the code may not apply to identifications that are made only a short time after the commission of an offence (*R v Kelly* (1992); *R v Hickin* (1996)).

Even where the code applies, failure to follow its provisions will not be fatal where to do so would be futile. Thus, a suspect who requests an identification parade will normally be entitled to one, but in *R v Montgomery* (1996) the Court of Appeal held that this was not the case where there was no reasonable possibility that a witness would be able to make an identification.

Code D contains provisions regulating the way in which identification by photographs should be made. But the fact that this means of identification has been adopted should not usually be brought out at trial by the prosecution because of what it will reveal about the defendant's background (*R v Lamb* (1980)).

# 10 Confessions and ill-gotten evidence

Although confessions are out of court statements adduced to prove the truth of their contents, they are admissible as an exception to the hearsay rule under s 76(1) of the Police and Criminal Evidence Act 1984 (PACE). But it is recognised that considerations of fairness or reliability may make it undesirable to admit evidence of a particular confession or of some other item of prosecution evidence. Sections 76 and 78 of PACE deal respectively with confessions and with a discretion to exclude, for reasons of fairness, evidence on which the prosecution proposes to rely. To try to secure reliability and fairness, Codes of Practice have been created under ss 60(1)(a) and 66 of PACE. These attempt to control the ways in which certain types of evidence are obtained, and breaches may lead to exclusion of an item of evidence under s 76 or s 78. The sections are often relied on in the alternative; in *R v Mason* (1988) it was held that s 78 applies to confessions as much as to any other kind of prosecution evidence.

By s 76(2), if in any proceedings:

- the prosecution proposes to give in evidence a confession made by an accused person; and

- it is represented to the court that the confession was or may have been obtained:

    (a) by oppression of the person who made it; or

    (b) in consequence of anything said or done which was likely, in the circumstances existing at the time, to

> render unreliable any confession which might be
> made by him in consequence thereof,

the court shall not allow the confession to be given in evidence *unless* the prosecution can prove that the confession (notwithstanding that it may be true) was *not* obtained in the circumstances referred to in (a) or (b) of the sub-section.

By sub-s (3), the court may of its own motion require the prosecution to satisfy it that a confession was not obtained in either of these circumstances.

By sub-s (4), the fact that a confession is wholly or partly excluded under sub-s (2) shall not affect the admissibility in evidence of any facts discovered as a result of the confession. By the same sub-section, where a confession has a relevance that goes beyond the truth of its contents, because it shows that the defendant speaks, writes or expresses himself in a particular way, so much of the confession as is necessary to show that he does so will be admissible.

## Recognising a confession

By s 82(1) of PACE, 'confession' includes any statement wholly or partly adverse to the person who made it, whether made to a person in authority or not, and whether made in words or otherwise. An apparently wholly exculpatory statement does not amount to a confession if it becomes adverse to its maker because it appears to be evasive, or because it is subsequently discovered to be false (*R v Sat-Bhambra* (1989)).

The partial definition in PACE assumes that a statement can be made by non-verbal means, and there are cases that suggest that an admission can be made by conduct. In *Moriarty v London, Chatham and Dover Rly Co* (1870) a plaintiff's attempts to persuade several persons to give false evidence in support of his claim was held to be evidence of an admission by conduct that the case he was putting forward was untrue. (See also *Parkes v R* (1976).) Even silence alone may amount to a confession if it can be construed as an adoption of an accusation by the person against whom it is made: see *Bessela v Stern* (1877), but cf *Wiedemann v Walpole* (1891). Also, in *R v Batt* (1995) the failure of one defendant to dissociate himself from incriminating observations made by his companion was held to amount to evidence against him as well as the speaker.

What one defendant says outside court not in the presence of a co-accused will be evidence against the speaker, but not against the co-accused (*R v Gunewardene* (1951)). But such a statement will not automatically be 'edited' at trial so as to exclude the parts that are inadmissible against a co-accused. The judge has a discretionary power to exclude relevant evidence on which the *prosecution* proposes to rely so as to ensure a fair trial, but this does not extend to the exculpatory part of a mixed statement on which a *defendant* proposes to rely, for example, in which he has put the blame on another defendant (*Lobban v The Queen* (1995)).

Note, however, that what one defendant says *when giving evidence in court* is evidence against a co-defendant whom it implicates (*R v Rudd* (1948)).

## Excluding a confession under s 76 of PACE 1984

Section 76(2)(a) provides for exclusion where the confession was, or may have been, obtained by oppression.

By s 76(8), oppression includes torture, inhuman or degrading treatment, and the use or threat of violence (whether or not amounting to torture). This is an inclusive, rather than an exclusive, definition. Further guidance can be obtained from *R v Fulling* (1987), in which Lord Lane said that the word should be given its ordinary dictionary meaning, viz:

> Exercise of authority or power in a burdensome, harsh or wrongful manner; unjust or cruel treatment of subjects, inferiors, etc; the imposition of unreasonable or unjust burdens.

But this quotation should not be read as if it were itself a statutory definition; the context makes it clear that Lord Lane was emphasising the seriousness of the conduct envisaged. However, physical violence, or the threat of it, are not essential elements. In *R v Paris* (1993) it was held that interviews had been oppressive where a suspect had been verbally bullied.

The statute excludes a confession which was or may have been *obtained by* oppression. It therefore remains theoretically possible that there could be an instance of oppression that does not in fact cause a particular confession to be made. In those circumstances the sub-section would not be available to the defence.

By s 76(2)(b) a confession will be excluded where it was, or may have been, obtained in consequence of anything said or done which was likely, in the circumstances existing at the time, to render unreliable any confession which might be made by the defendant in consequence thereof. The test is therefore one of *hypothetical* rather than *actual* reliability: see *R v Cox* (1991).

With s 76(2)(b), as with s 76(2)(a), a causative link between the matters complained of and a confession must be shown, at least as a possibility, before there can be exclusion. The usual approach to s 76(2)(b) has been to say that 'anything said or done' had to refer to something said or done by some person other than the suspect: see, for example, *R v Goldenberg* (1989). But in *R v Walker* (1998) the Court of Appeal appears to have taken the view that the mere interviewing of a suspect is capable of being something 'said or done' for the purposes of this provision. Even if the line taken in *R v Walker* were not to be followed, there would still be room for a submission in favour of exclusion to be made under s 78 where the factors making for unreliability stemmed solely from the suspect who made the confession (*R v Anderson* (1993)). And even on the pre-*Walker* approach, once you could show an external factor making for unreliability, it was then open to the court to take into account the personal circumstances of the person making the confession, because they are part of the 'circumstances existing at the time' which, by s 76(2)(b), are to be taken into account when considering reliability (see, for example, *R v McGovern* (1993)).

Where a defendant has made an admission that is vulnerable to s 76 at a first interview, a similar admission at a later interview may also be capable of being attacked, even though the original vitiating elements are no longer present, because the very fact of having made an earlier admission is likely to have an effect on the later interview (*R v McGovern* (1993)).

Confessions obtained after breach of a suspect's right to legal advice have very often been excluded. The right, which is set out in s 58 of PACE, is regarded as 'one of the most important and fundamental rights of a citizen' (*R v Samuel* (1988)). The case of *R v Alladice* (1988) was decided on its own exceptional facts, which included an admission by the defendant on the voir dire that he was well able to cope with police interviews and had asked for a solicitor only to have a check on police conduct. It remains to be seen whether the availability of legal advice will retain its old importance now that inferences may be drawn from a suspect's exercise of his right to silence under the Criminal Justice and Public Order Act 1994.

### Section 76 at a glance
### Section 76(2)(a)

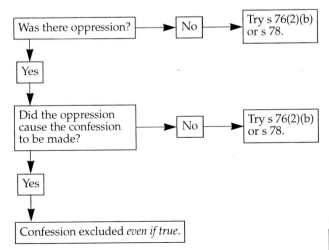

## Section 76(2)(b)

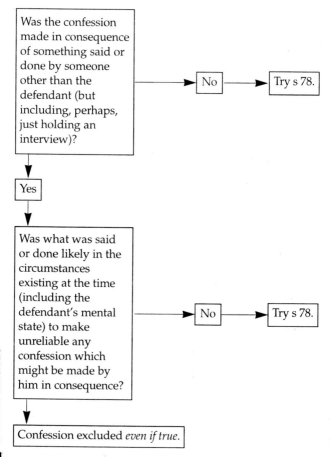

Was the confession made in consequence of something said or done by someone other than the defendant (but including, perhaps, just holding an interview)? → No → Try s 78.

Yes

Was what was said or done likely in the circumstances existing at the time (including the defendant's mental state) to make unreliable any confession which might be made by him in consequence? → No → Try s 78.

Confession excluded *even if true.*

**Section 78(1) of PACE 1984**

This sub-section provides that in any proceedings the court may refuse to allow evidence on which the prosecution proposes to rely to be given if it appears to the court that, having regard to all the circumstances, including the circumstances in which the evidence was obtained, the admission of the evidence would have such an adverse effect on the fairness of the proceedings that the court ought not to admit it.

The following points of interpretation should be noted:

- the evidence must be evidence on which the prosecution *proposes* to rely; it is too late to use the sub-section if the evidence has already been given (*R v Sat-Bhambra* (1989));

- it is not enough that the admission of the evidence will have *some* adverse effect; the adverse effect must be so great that the court ought not to admit the evidence (*R v Walsh* (1990)). However, once that stage has been reached, the judge must exclude the evidence – despite the use of 'may' in the opening words of the sub-section (*R v Chalkley* (1998));

- the 'fairness of the proceedings' refers only to that part of the proceedings taking place in court (*R v Mason* (1988));

- it is fairness of the proceedings that the judge has to consider. Fairness to the defendant is part of this idea, but so is fairness to the prosecution (*R v Robb* (1991)).

## The exercise of the discretion

The Court of Appeal has given trial judges a very free hand in their operation of s 78(1) and has subjected their decisions to a minimum of review. In *R v Samuel* (1988) the Court of Appeal said it was undesirable to attempt any general guidance as to the way in which a judge's discretion under s 78 should be exercised, and in *R v Jelen* (1989) and *R v Roberts* (1997) the Court of Appeal made the same point, saying that this was not an apt field for hard case law and well founded distinctions between cases.

Recent obiter dicta of Auld LJ in *R v Chalkley* (1998) suggest that the scope of a judge's powers under s 78 may be less wide than appears from earlier cases, and, in particular, may not extend to those cases where the evidence, though unlawfully or improperly obtained, is still reliable. It remains to be seen whether these remarks become generally accepted as the proper interpretation of s 78(1).

Several cases show that the Court of Appeal will interfere with a trial judge's exercise of his discretion under s 78(1) only for '*Wednesbury* unreasonableness': see, for example, *R v Christou* (1992); *R v McEvoy* (1997).

In *Vel v Owen* (1987) the Divisional Court held that the prosecution does not have a burden under the sub-section to disprove unfairness in the way that it has a burden to disprove the existence of vitiating circumstances under s 76. But in *R v Anderson* (1993) the Court of Appeal said that it was not entirely clear where the burden of proof lay on all the issues raised by the sub-section, and in *R v Stagg* (1994) prosecuting counsel accepted that it was for the prosecution to demonstrate either that there was no unfairness, or that its degree did not warrant the exclusion of the evidence.

A breach of one of the Codes of Practice may help to get evidence excluded under s 78(1). As the Court of Appeal said in *R v Elson* (1994), the Codes exist to protect the individual against the might of the State. The court added that the individual is at a great disadvantage when arrested by the police, and this is so whether or not the police have behaved with the utmost propriety. But breach of the codes will not lead to automatic exclusion of evidence (*R v Keenan* (1989); *R v Kelly* (1998)).

Even evidence obtained by a trick, or during an undercover operation, may be admissible (*R v Bailey* (1993), but cf *R v Mason* (1988)). In *R v Smurthwaite* (1994) the Court of Appeal listed some of the factors to be regarded when considering the admissibility of evidence obtained during an undercover operation:

- Was the officer acting as an *agent provocateur* in the sense that he was enticing a defendant to commit an offence he would not otherwise have committed?

- What was the nature of the entrapment?

- Does the evidence consist of admissions to a completed offence, or does it consist of the actual commission of an offence?

- How active or passive was the officer's role in obtaining the evidence?

- Is there an unassailable record of what occurred, or is there strong supporting evidence?

- Did the officer abuse his undercover role to ask questions which ought properly to have been asked as a police officer, and in accordance with the codes?

## The common law discretion to exclude

The effect of s 82(3) of PACE is to retain the common law discretion to exclude evidence on the ground that its probative value is outweighed by its likely prejudicial effect. This is the discretion that operates in relation to the prosecution's right to cross-examine under s 1(f)(ii) of the Criminal Evidence Act 1898. Although potentially available in other circumstances, this is the only area where it is much used.

## Use of confessions by a co-defendant

Where a defendant's confession has been excluded under s 76 or s 78 of PACE, it is no longer available for the prosecution to use. But in *R v Myers* (1997) the House of Lords suggested that such a confession may be available for use by a co-defendant. The confession must be relevant in some way to the co-defendant's case. There is a second condition that applies, the scope of which is not yet clear. It is that the confession must not have been obtained in circumstances rendering it unreliable or involuntary. (The scope of *Myers* is difficult to state because the trial judge in that case never got round to ruling the relevant confession inadmissible: the prosecution just accepted that they ought not to use it because it had been obtained in breach of the Code of Practice.)

## Failure to answer questions or mention facts

Under the Criminal Justice and Public Order Act 1994 (CJPOA) there may be circumstances in which a suspect's silence, though not amounting to a confession, may be used as the basis for making inferences at trial.

### Section 34 of the CJPOA 1994

A court or jury may draw such inferences as appear proper from evidence that the defendant failed, on being questioned under caution or on being charged with the offence, to mention any fact relied on in his defence if it was a fact which, in the circumstances existing at the time, he could reasonably have been expected to mention. The section applies to questioning by police officers, but also to questioning by other persons charged with the duty of investigating offences or charging offenders (s 34(4)).

When deciding whether a defendant could reasonably have been expected to mention a particular fact, consideration has to be taken of the *actual* defendant, with such qualities, knowledge, apprehensions and advice as he or she had at the time (*R v Argent* (1997)).

If a defendant says he refused to answer questions on legal advice, that by itself is unlikely to be a sufficient reason for his failure to mention facts subsequently relied on in his defence. In practice, a defendant will have to go further and provide, either through his own testimony or that of his legal adviser, the reasons for the advice (*R v Condron* (1997)).

### Sections 36 and 37 of the CJPOA 1994

These sections deal with inferences that may be drawn, in certain circumstances, from a defendant's failure to account for objects, substances, marks or his own presence in a particular place.

## Inferences from refusal to provide samples

By s 62(10) of PACE, an adverse inference may be drawn from a suspect's refusal, without good cause, to consent to the taking of 'intimate samples' from his body. By s 65 of

PACE (as amended by the CJPOA 1994) an 'intimate sample' is:

- a sample of blood, semen or any other tissue fluid, urine or pubic hair;

- a dental impression;

- a swab taken from a person's body orifice other than the mouth.

'Non-intimate samples' may be taken, subject to procedural conditions, without a suspect's consent, and no provision corresponding to s 62(10) is therefore necessary.

# 11 Similar fact evidence

## Nature and development of the law

Similar fact evidence is evidence that one party wants to adduce as part of its case against another party:

- to show that other party to be guilty of some misconduct other than that primarily alleged in the proceedings; or

- to show that other party to have some discreditable propensity or interest.

It differs from simple evidence of bad character in that it goes to an issue in the case *other than* the mere credibility of the person against whom it is adduced. Thus, its admissibility does not depend on whether the opposing party chooses to testify or not.

The expression 'similar fact evidence' was adopted because problems of admissibility typically arose where a defendant was alleged to have committed a crime in an unusual way, and where there was evidence to show that the defendant had behaved similarly on previous occasions. But the problem is not confined to such situations and can also arise, for example, where articles of an incriminating nature are found in the defendant's possession, or where the defendant admits having an interest in something (for example, paedophilia) that may be relevant to the charge alleged against him.

Most of the law about similar fact evidence is to be found in criminal cases because of the danger that a jury hearing such evidence may be prejudiced against the defendant in at least one of two ways:

(a) 'reasoning prejudice' may lead them to conclude that the evidence has more weight than in fact is the case;

(b) 'moral prejudice' may lead them to conclude that the defendant is an undesirable character who ought to be put in prison for society's protection, regardless of whether he is actually guilty of the current offence for which he is being tried.

Similar fact problems rarely arise in civil proceedings, the vast majority of which are tried by a judge alone, who is thought to be able to resist the prejudices of ordinary people like jurors. Normally, therefore, a civil court will admit similar fact evidence wherever it is relevant in determining the matters in issue, provided it would not be oppressive or unfair to the other side (*Mood Music Publishing Co Ltd v De Wolfe Publishing Ltd* (1976)); but on the rare occasions where a civil case is heard by a judge and a jury, the stricter approach of the criminal courts will be adopted (*Thorpe v Chief Constable of Greater Manchester Police* (1989)).

The foundation of the modern approach in criminal cases is the speech by Lord Herschell in *Makin v AG for New South Wales* (1894), in which he laid down two principles:

- the prosecution may not adduce evidence tending to show that the defendant is guilty of criminal acts other than those for which he is being currently tried *for the purpose of leading to the conclusion that the defendant is a person likely from his criminal character to have committed the offence in the present indictment;*

- but the mere fact that evidence tends to show the commission of other offences does not make it inadmissible *if it is relevant to an issue in the current trial*, for example, if the evidence in question goes to rebut a defence that would be open to the defendant.

Although for some decades after *Makin* the courts interpreted what Lord Herschell had said in a mechanical way, it has been clear since *DPP v Boardman* (1975) that admissibility of similar fact evidence is governed by a balancing exercise, in which the judge weighs on the one hand the probative worth of the evidence, and, on the other, its likely prejudicial effect (in the terms referred to above of 'reasoning' and 'moral' prejudice).

Although 'striking similarity' between the facts of the current offence and the similar fact evidence may well provide sufficient probative worth to tip the balance in favour of admissibility, striking similarity is not an absolute require-ment. The starting point is, of course, the relevance of the proposed evidence; then comes the question: what is its weight? There is no single way of assessing such weight (*DPP v P* (1991); *R v Groves* (1998)).

## Proof and similar fact evidence

Any presentation of similar fact cases runs the risk of appearing to classify the subject matter into a system of rules and exceptions, governed by precedent. This was the mistake made by the courts before *Boardman*, and even to some extent up to *DPP v P*. In *R v Kidd* (1995), the Court of Appeal acknowledged that *DPP v P* has considerably enlarged the scope of similar fact evidence. However, some examples of its modern use may be useful.

### To prove motive

In *R v Williams* (1987) the defendant was charged, under s 16 of the Offences Against the Person Act 1861, with making a threat to kill. The section required the prosecution to prove the threat had been made with the intention that the person threatened would fear that the threat would be carried out.

Evidence of previous threatening and violent conduct by the defendant towards the victim was held admissible because it helped to prove this intention.

**To prove identification**

Similar fact evidence can be used to support an eye witness' identification. For example, evidence of earlier misconduct by the defendant may help to do this, and so may the defendant's possession of incriminating articles.

Where earlier misconduct is relied on, two slightly different approaches have been adopted. In the 'sequential' approach, illustrated by *R v McGranaghan* (1995), the judge first decides whether the crime for which the defendant is being tried and the other misconduct are 'strikingly similar'. If he thinks that they are, the jury must consider whether the current offence and the other misconduct were committed by the same person. If their answer is 'Yes', they must next ask whether the defendant committed the other misconduct. If the answer to that is 'Yes', it will follow that the defendant is guilty of the offence charged.

Where the other misconduct is the subject of other counts in the same indictment, as in *R v Barnes* (1995), the court is likely to adopt the 'pooling' approach. Here the first question for the jury is whether the same person committed all the offences charged. If their answer to that is 'Yes', they may then add together evidence relevant to the issue of identity from each count in order to establish the identity of the culprit. If the accumulated evidence points to the defendant, it follows that he is guilty on all counts.

Although striking similarity will often provide the necessary probative weight to support an identification, other types of evidence may do so. Sometimes sufficient probative worth has been found in the possession of incriminating articles by the defendant. The old case of *Thompson v R* (1918) is possibly capable of being supported on this basis, but *R v Taylor* (1923) is authority for the proposition that the articles found must have had some connection with the crime charged.

**To rebut a defence**
Similar fact evidence has often been admitted to rebut a defence that the defendant had no criminal intent. For example, such evidence was admitted in *R v Mortimer* (1936) to show that the defendant had intentionally run down his victim in a motor car, and in *R v Kidd* (1995) to show that the defendant did not have a metal detector with him for the innocent purpose that he claimed.

Often, where the defence amounts to the denial of the *actus reus*, similar fact evidence has been held inadmissible. So, for example, in *R v B* (1997) where allegations of sexual offences were made by schoolboys against their head master, and his defence was that their stories were fabricated, the Court of Appeal held that evidence should not have been admitted of articles found in his possession that merely tended to show he had homosexual inclinations. However, evidence of inclination may be admitted where the *actus reus* is admitted, but the defence is that it was done with innocent intent. This was the case in *R v Lewis* (1983), where the defendant (who had paedophile interests) admitted accidentally touching a child and drying a child after a bath.

Recent cases have shown that what a defendant says in a police interview to support his denial of an offence may well lead to the admissibility of similar fact evidence. In *R v Da Silva* (1990), the defendant explained his possession of a dagger that looked like the one used in a robbery, by claiming that it was part of his equipment for martial arts training. To throw doubt on this explanation, the prosecution were allowed to prove that police had also discovered, hidden under floorboards, at premises occupied by the defendant, a meat cleaver, a knife and a truncheon. This was so, even though there was no evidence that these items had been used in the robbery.

It seems clear that similar fact evidence will be readily admitted in drug importation cases. Thus, in *R v Sokialiois* (1993) possession of a quantity of drugs not the subject of the charge was held admissible to rebut the claim made by the defendant to the police that he didn't even take drugs, on the basis that that claim had been made to support the defence that the drugs that were the subject of the charge had been planted on him. And, in *R v Peters* (1995), where the defendant was charged with an importation offence, the Court of Appeal said (obiter) that evidence of finding at the defendant's home small quantities of cannabis and some drug-related equipment would have been admissible to rebut a claim that he did not know how a quantity of amphetamines had come to be concealed in his car. In *R v Groves* (1998), a charge of being knowingly concerned in the importation of cannabis, the prosecution were allowed to rebut a defence of innocent association with the co-defendants by showing the defendant's possession of cash and cannabis.

## The possibility of collusion between witnesses

In *R v H* (1995), the House of Lords said that as a general rule, where an application is made to admit similar fact evidence, the judge should decide the question on the assumption that the facts alleged are true, and should normally ignore any allegation that there may have been collusion between witnesses. Save in exceptional circumstances, the question of collusion is a matter for the jury alone. But where it is raised as an issue by the defence, the judge should direct the jury that they must be satisfied the similar fact evidence is free from collusion before it can be relied on to support the prosecution case.

## Section 27(3) of the Theft Act 1968

This sub-section applies where a person is being proceeded against only for handling stolen goods. Its effect is that if evidence has been given:

- of his having or arranging to have in his possession the goods that are the subjects of the charge; or

- of his undertaking or assisting in, or arranging to undertake or assist in, their retention, removal, disposal or realisation,

certain evidence shall be admissible, *but only for the purpose of proving that he knew or believed the goods to be stolen goods.*

That evidence can be of two kinds:

(a) evidence that he has had in his possession, or has undertaken or assisted in the retention, removal, disposal or realisation of, stolen goods from any theft taking place not earlier than 12 months before the offence charged. This permits evidence of a possession *later* than the offence charged (*R v Davies* (1972)). NB: the mere fact of possession is enough; there is no need for the defendant to have been prosecuted in relation to the earlier incident;

(b) evidence that he has within the five years preceding the date of the offence charged been convicted of theft or handling. If the prosecution want to use this information, they must give the defendant seven days' notice in writing of their intention.

Unlike the common law test for the admissibility of similar fact evidence, the sub-section makes no provision for balancing the probative worth of the evidence against its prejudicial effect. But a judge can still take this into account, because what is admissible in principle under the sub-section can still be excluded in the judge's discretion, either at common law or under s 78 of PACE (*R v Hacker* (1994)).

### Similar fact evidence and co-defendants

The test for admitting similar fact evidence itself involves a balancing of probative worth and prejudicial effect. In principle, therefore, there should be no difference in the test applied where a co-defendant, rather than the prosecution, wishes to call similar fact evidence in an attempt to shift the blame from himself to his companion in the dock. But the position has been bedevilled by some judges who still talk as if a judge applying the common law test for admissibility had, in adddition, a discretion to exclude similar fact evidence because its prejudicial effect exceeded its probative worth: see, for example, *R v Lunt* (1986); *R v Burns* (1996). If that were right, the position of a defendant who made an application to admit similar fact evidence would be stronger than that of a prosecutor, because a judge has no discretion to exclude admissible evidence called by one defendant on the ground that it has the effect of prejudicing another (*R v Lobban* (1995)).

# 12 Character evidence

Evidence about character may be relevant in either a civil or criminal trial in two ways:

(a) it may be relevant to an issue in the case;

(b) it may be relevant to a witness' credibility.

Traditionally, English law has operated on the basis that a conviction for any offence is relevant to credibility: see, for example, *Clifford v Clifford* (1961). In practice, this approach is not always adopted. In particular, there are two restrictions that apply to witnesses generally in respect of cross-examination about previous convictions.

In *Hobbs v Tinling* (1929) Sankey LJ said that a question as to credit will be:

- *proper* if the information that the question is designed to elicit would seriously affect the court's opinion as to the credibility of the witness on the matter to which he is testifying;

- *improper* if designed to elicit information about matters so remote in time, or of such a character, that the truth of the imputation would not affect, or would affect only in a slight degree, the opinion of the court about the witness' credibility on the matter to which he is testifying.

Section 1(1) of the Rehabilitation of Offenders Act, allows a person's convictions to be 'spent' after a certain period of time has gone by. Where a person's convictions are spent, there is a general prohibition under s 4(1) against referring to them in judicial proceedings. This prohibition is limited by s 7(2), which in effect gives free scope for reference to spent convictions in criminal proceedings. But in a *Practice Direction* (1975) Lord Widgery CJ stated that no one should refer in open court to a spent conviction without the authority of the judge, and he should not give authority unless the interests of justice require it. The effect of s 7(3) of the Act is that spent convictions may be referred to in a civil trial, subject to the judge's discretion, where credit is in issue and the convictions are relevant to credit (*Thomas v Commissioner of Police of the Metropolis* (1997)).

## Evidence of good character in criminal proceedings

There are limitations on the sort of evidence that can be adduced for the purpose of showing that a defendant, because of his good character, is unlikely to be guilty. Under the rule in *R v Rowton* (1865), only evidence of general reputation is admissible as evidence of good character. (This includes the fact that the defendant has no previous convictions.) Evidence of the opinions of specific persons, and evidence of specific good acts performed by the defendant are inadmissible. In practice, judges do not always keep strictly to these rules, but it is clear from *R v Redgrave* (1981) that any relaxation of the rule is an indulgence by the court, and not a defendant's right.

## The significance of good character

Where evidence of good character is given, its significance must be explained to the jury. Any judicial direction is now governed by rules laid down by the Court of Appeal in *R v Vye* (1993). This case recognised two 'limbs' in any direction about good character:

- the relevance of good character to credibility;
- the relevance of good character to the question of guilt or innocence ('propensity').

In addition, the court laid down the following rules to deal with various problem cases:

- when a defendant has not given evidence at trial, but relies in support of his defence on exculpatory statements made to police or others, the judge should tell the jury to have regard to the defendant's good character when considering the credibility of those statements;

- the second limb of the direction must always be given where the defendant is of good character. For these purposes, no distinction is drawn between defendants who have testified and those who have not. The judge should indicate that good character is relevant to propensity, but the actual words used are a matter for the judge in each case;

- a defendant of good character is entitled to a full direction, even if jointly tried with someone of bad character. In dealing with a co-defendant of bad character a judge may *either* say nothing at all on the subject, *or* tell the jury that they have heard nothing about the co-defendant's character, and that they must not speculate about that or use it as evidence against him.

**Doubtful cases of good character**

Sometimes a defendant will admit, as part of his defence, to *some* wrongdoing, though not that alleged by the prosecution. If he has no previous convictions, the *Vye* directions should usually still be given, subject to whatever qualification the judge thinks appropriate (*R v Aziz* (1996)). When a defendant has already pleaded guilty to some counts on an indictment, but is contesting others, the earlier pleas will generally mean that he is no longer of good character. Any direction about character in such a case will be a matter for the judge's discretion (*R v Challenger* (1994)).

**Spent convictions and good character**

With the leave of the judge, a defendant with spent convictions can be presented as a person of good character, provided the jury is not misled (*R v Bailey* (1989)). He can therefore be described as, for example, 'a man of good character with no relevant convictions'. Even if a conviction is not spent, it may be similarly overlooked if it is minor and of no significance in the context of the current charge (*R v H* (1994)). If an earlier conviction is ignored, or, though mentioned, treated as irrelevant, the judge should give the *Vye* directions (*R v H* (1994)).

## Evidence of bad character in criminal proceedings

Where the defendant is of bad character, the prosecution may be able to introduce this as similar fact evidence. If they cannot do this, evidence of a defendant's bad character may still be adduced as a result of the way in which his defence is run. So far as defence witnesses other than the defendant are concerned, the only legal restrictions on cross-examining them about their previous convictions are contained in the rule in *Hobbs v Tinling* and in the Rehabilitation of Offenders Act and the 1975 *Practice Direction*. (There may be relevant rules of professional etiquette that an advocate will have to consider as well.)

**The defendant's position at common law**

This will apply only where the defendant does not give evidence. The rule, stated in *R v Butterwasser* (1948), is that if he puts his character in issue, *either* by calling evidence of his own good character, *or* by cross-examining prosecution witnesses to that effect, evidence in rebuttal can be called by the prosecution to show that the defendant is in fact of bad character. But a defendant does not, at common law, put his own character in issue by cross-examining prosecution witnesses to show that *they* are of bad character. In such a case the prosecution cannot call evidence about the defendant's bad character.

## The defendant's position under the Criminal Evidence Act 1898

Section 1(e) removes from the defendant the ordinary witness' privilege against self-incrimination by providing that a defendant who gives evidence may be asked any question in cross-examination 'notwithstanding that it would tend to criminate him as to the offence charged'. Section 1(f) restricts the prosecution's right to cross-examine a witness who is a defendant about previous convictions. In *Jones v DPP* (1962) the House of Lords held that sub-s (f) always prevails over sub-s (e), so that, if cross-examination tends to show that the defendant has committed other offences than those charged, it can be permitted only in the circumstances set out in provisos (i), (ii) or (iii). But the case also decided that the cross-examination prohibited under s 1(f) is cross-examination that tends to show the jury *for the first time* that the defendant has committed another offence.

### The opening words of sub-s (f)

'Charged' means 'accused before a court', and not merely suspected, or accused but not prosecuted (*Stirland v DPP* (1944)).

The word 'charged' is capable of letting in questions about a previous *acquittal*, but such evidence would have to be relevant, and this could be difficult to establish (*Maxwell v DPP* (1935)).

'Character' refers to reputation and disposition (*Stirland v DPP* (1944)). Thus, in theory, the prosecution could cross-examine a defendant who had lost the protection of the statute about discreditable acts which were not the subject of any criminal prosecution (*R v Carter* (1997)).

### Section 1(f)(i) of the Criminal Evidence Act 1898

This applies where proof that the defendant has committed or been convicted of another offence is admissible evidence to show that he is guilty of the offence charged. It follows that cross-examination under s 1(f)(i) is relevant to the defendant's guilt as well as to his credibility.

Cross-examination under this proviso is limited by its own wording to cases where the prosecution wish to prove that the defendant has *committed* or *been convicted of* an earlier offence. Thus under this proviso cross-examination about previous acquittals is not permissible (*R v Cokar* (1960)).

### Section 1(f)(ii) of the Criminal Evidence Act 1898

There are two ways in which a s 1(f)(ii) situation can arise:

- by the defendant's attempting to establish his own good character, either by cross-examining prosecution witnesses to that effect, or by giving evidence himself of his good character, or by calling character witnesses ('first limb' of the sub-section);

- where the nature or conduct of the defence is such as to involve imputations on the character of a prosecution witness or the deceased victim of the alleged crime ('second limb' of the sub-section).

(But NB: s 1(f)(ii) applies only where the defendant himself gives evidence. Otherwise, the common law applies.)

### The first limb
A defendant who gives evidence will have to counter the prosecution's version of events. He will not put his own character in issue by that alone. He will do so where what he says goes beyond his need to meet the facts alleged by the prosecution, so as to raise the issue of his good character as an independent reason for acquitting him (*Malindi v The Queen* (1967)).

Character is said to be 'indivisible'. This means that if a defendant puts any aspect of his character in issue, the prosecution is entitled to refer to the whole of his character. Thus, in *R v Winfield* (1939) it was held that a defendant charged with indecently assaulting a woman could be cross-examined about previous convictions for dishonesty after calling a witness to establish his good character in relation to sexual morality. (See also *R v Marsh* (1994).)

For the purpose of this proviso, a witness for the prosecution includes, as well as those giving oral evidence in court, witnesses whose evidence is admitted as documentary hearsay under ss 23 or 24 of the Criminal Justice Act 1988, or a witness whose statement is read under s 9 of the Criminal Justice Act 1967 (*R v Miller* (1997)).

The proviso applies even where the imputation is a necessary part of the defence, save that in rape cases the defendant will not bring himself within the proviso merely by alleging that the complainant consented to intercourse (*Selvey v DPP* (1970)).

In deciding whether an imputation has been made, it is vital to look not just at the words used, but at the context in which they have been used. If what a defendant says amounts in reality to no more than a denial of the charge in emphatic language, it should not be regarded as coming within the proviso (*R v Rouse* (1904); *Selvey v DPP* (1970)). But an imputation can be made politely, and that will be caught. Thus, if what is alleged amounts in effect to an allegation that a witness is telling a deliberate falsehood, the proviso will come into operation (*R v Britzman* (1983)).

**The extent of questioning under s 1(f)(ii)**

This was recently considered by the Court of Appeal in *R v McLeod* (1994), where the following propositions (among others) were stated:

- the purpose of cross-examination under s 1(f)(ii) is to show that the defendant is not worthy of belief, not to show that he has a disposition to commit the type of offence with which he is charged. But the mere fact that the earlier convictions are for offences similar to that charged will not make cross-examination improper;

- unless the earlier offences are relied on as similar fact evidence, prosecuting counsel should not try to bring out similarities between the underlying facts of previous offences and those of the current offence;

- two specific lines of questioning may be relevant to credibility;

  (a) questions about similar defences (for example, false alibis or allegations that incriminating substances had been planted) which have been rejected by juries on previous occasions;

  (b) questions about whether the defendant pleaded not guilty and gave evidence on the earlier occasions;

- in every case where there has been cross-examination under s 1(f)(ii) the judge must, in summing up, warn the jury that the questioning goes only to credit, and not to the defendant's propensity to commit the offence they are considering.

**Judicial discretion to exclude s 1(f)(ii) cross-examination**

The judge has a common law discretion, preserved by PACE, to exclude evidence whose probative worth is outweighed by its likely prejudicial effect. It is in relation to prosecution cross-examination under s 1(f)(ii) that this discretion is now chiefly used. Current guidelines, based on earlier cases, appear in *R v Owen* (1985), and can be summarised as follows:

- when it is clear that a s 1(f)(ii) situation has arisen, the judge must weigh the prejudicial effect of the proposed questions against the damage done by the attack on the prosecution witness, and must generally exercise his discretion so as to secure a trial that is fair to both prosecution and defence;

- the general principle is that the jury should know about the character of the man who is saying things to the discredit of the prosecution witness;

- the fact that the defendant's previous convictions are not for offences of dishonesty, or may be for offences closely resembling the offence charged, are matters to be taken into consideration, but they do not oblige the judge to disallow the cross-examination.

These guidelines assume a situation where the second limb of s 1(f)(ii) is relied on. Situations where the defendant is caught by the first limb are relatively rare; presumably similar considerations would be applied. In *R v Owen* the

EVIDENCE

Court of Appeal also said that it would not interfere with a judge's exercise of discretion unless he had erred in principle or there was no material on which he could properly have reached his decision. A case that may show a more interventionist approach is *R v Davison-Jenkins* (1997), where the Court of Appeal said of a defendant charged with shoplifting that it had been effectively impossible for the jury to disregard propensity once it had been revealed under s 1(f)(ii) cross-examination that she had previous convictions for shoplifting.

### Section 1(f)(iii) of the Criminal Evidence Act 1898

Under this provision, a defendant who gives evidence may be questioned about the matters referred to in the opening words of s 1(f) where he has given evidence against any other person charged in the same proceedings. The leading case of *Murdoch v Taylor* (1965) established that:

- the motive that may have prompted the giving of such evidence is irrelevant;

- there is no discretion to disallow cross-examination under this proviso by counsel for a co-defendant. But counsel for the prosecution might want to use the proviso, and then the judge does have a discretion to refuse leave;

- the evidence against the co-defendant may be given in chief or during cross-examination;

- the relevance of such cross-examination is to credit only.

In *Murdoch v Taylor* the House of Lords said that 'evidence against' a co-defendant for the purpose of this proviso was evidence which, taken in the context of the whole case, supports the prosecution's case or undermines the defence of the co-defendant. Later cases have elaborated this basic proposition as follows:

- for the evidence of one defendant to support the prosecution case so as to bring s 1(f)(iii) into operation, it must do so in relation to a matter that is in contest between the prosecution and the co-defendant (*R v Crawford* (1998)).

- where the evidence of one defendant, if believed, inevitably entails the guilt of another, the proviso will apply (*R v Varley* (1982); cf *R v Bruce* (1975); *R v Kirkpatrick* (1998));

- but s 1(f)(iii) may apply where the evidence of one defendant, while not entailing the guilt of another, makes that other's testimony less credible (*R v Crawford* (1998)).

Just as the details of previous offences may be relevant to credibility under s 1(f)(ii), so they may be under s 1(f)(iii) (*R v Reid* (1989)).

**Cross-examination of a co-defendant at common law**
Cross-examination of a co-defendant is not solely governed by s 1(f)(iii) of the 1898 Act. An advocate for one defendant may need to bring out matters to the discredit of another defendant in support of his own client's case, both during examination-in-chief and during cross-examination. This is permissible, provided the judge is satisfied that the matters are relevant. Once satisfied of this, the judge has no discretion to exclude the evidence (*R v Miller* (1952); *R v Bracewell* (1978)).

## Summary of differences between common law and 1898 Act

| Action of defendant with previous convictions | Common law | Criminal Evidence Act 1898 |
|---|---|---|
| Gives evidence of his own good character | N/A | Caught by s 1(f)(ii) |
| Calls character witness | Prosecution can call evidence in rebuttal | Caught by s 1(f)(ii) |
| Cross-examines prosecution witness to establish own good character | Prosecution can call evidence in rebuttal | Caught by s 1(f)(ii) |
| Casts imputation on prosecution witness by cross-examination | Prosecution can do nothing | Caught by s 1(f)(ii) |
| Casts imputation on prosecution witness during own evidence-in-chief | N/A | Caught by s 1(f)(ii) |
| Gives evidence against a co-accused | N/A | Caught by s 1(f)(iii) |

**Figure 12.1**

# 13 Opinion evidence

The main topics of importance are: (1) the circumstances in which opinion evidence is generally admissible; (2) analysing the basis on which an opinion has been given; and (3) the extent to which the evidence of psychiatrists or psychologists is admissible in criminal trials.

## When is opinion evidence admissible?

The fundamental rule is that witnesses testify about facts and not about the opinions they have formed from facts. The reason for this is the idea that it is the job of the 'tribunal of fact' (a judge or, very occasionally, a jury in a civil case, and magistrates or a jury in a criminal case) to hear the evidence, find facts, and make inferences from them. For this reason a witness should not generally be asked to give his opinion about what another witness has said (*R v Windass* (1989)).

By s 3(2) of the Civil Evidence Act 1972, a person called as a witness in civil proceedings may give a statement of opinion on any matter on which he is not qualified to give expert evidence, if that statement is made as a way of conveying relevant facts personally perceived by him.

The main exception to the fundamental rule is that in both civil and criminal cases an expert may give evidence of his opinion where the matters on which he testifies are likely to be outside the experience of judge or jury. In *R v Stockwell* (1993) the Court of Appeal said that in each case it is for the judge to decide:

- whether the issue is one on which the court could be assisted by expert evidence;

- whether the expert tendered has the expertise to provide such evidence.

While a witness giving such evidence should be skilled in the subject, there are no restrictions on the manner in which that skill has to be acquired. The evidence of a person without professional qualifications can be admitted provided the judge is satisfied that the witness is sufficiently skilled (*R v Silverlock* (1894)). So a witness who has acquired his expertise in the course of his daily work may give expert evidence even though he lacks paper qualifications. See, for example, *R v Murphy* (1980), where a police constable who was a traffic accident expert was allowed to give evidence of his opinion as to the nature of a collision, the course of one of the vehicles involved and other matters said to be deducible from marks in the road and damage to the vehicles.

A witness who is otherwise not specially qualified may be an 'expert *ad hoc*' where he has special knowledge acquired by study of materials that are relevant in a particular case, such as video recordings or photographs (*R v Clare & Peach* (1995)).

Although it is clear that the object of expert evidence is to provide the court with information that is outside the experience of judge or jury, there is little authority on how to determine whether particular information falls within this class. A case where a problem did arise (though it was not the central problem) was *R v Stagg* (1994), where the trial judge doubted whether evidence obtained from the technique known as 'psychological profiling' was expert evidence of a kind recognised by the courts.

## The basis of the opinion

An expert gives his opinion on the basis of facts in a particular case but those facts must themselves be proved by admissible evidence. However, if the rule against hearsay were strictly applied an expert would often be prevented from giving an opinion because his reasoning and conclusions will be governed by matters that he has learned in the course of his training and experience, either from what he has read or from others who share his specialisation. The courts have therefore relaxed the hearsay rule to take this into account (*Abbey National Mortgages plc v Key Surveyors Nationwide Ltd* (1996)).

Experts may support their opinions by referring to articles, letters to journals and other materials, whether published or not, when giving their testimony. Where they have done so, however, this should be mentioned in their evidence so that it can be taken into account when considering the probative worth of their opinion as a whole (*R v Abadom* (1983)).

Sometimes the primary facts of a case are not established by the expert himself, but by other members of a team, which the expert leads. In such a case, the evidence of the other relevant team members must be available (in the absence of formal admissions), so that the primary facts can all be proved by admissible evidence (*R v Jackson* (1996)).

By s 30(1) of the Criminal Justice Act 1988, an 'expert report' (that is, a written report by a person dealing wholly or mainly with matters on which he is, or, if living, would be, qualified to give expert evidence) shall be admissible as evidence in criminal proceedings, whether or not the person making it attends to give oral evidence. If it is proposed that the person making the report shall not give oral evidence, the report shall be admissible only with leave of the court (but it seems most unlikely that a court would allow an expert report to be adduced without calling the maker if the opposing party had a genuine desire to cross-examine on it).

## Evidence from psychiatrists and psychologists

To some extent judges recognise that a psychiatrist or psychologist may be able to provide useful testimony about matters that are outside the experience of judge or jurors (see, for example, *DPP v A & BC Chewing Gum Ltd* (1968), which concerned the effect of certain articles on children and *R v Morris* (1998), in which the Court of Appeal held that expert evidence is required where it is alleged that psychiatric illness or injury resulted from a defendant's non-physical assault).

But there is also a fear that mental experts will usurp the role of the jury or other triers of fact unless a clear line is drawn between abnormal and normal mental states. One effect of this has been to draw a distinction between expert evidence relevant to the reliability of a confession and expert evidence relevant to *mens rea*. Judges regularly admit psychiatric or psychological evidence when considering submissions about the admissibility of confessions, because the mental condition of the defendant at the time of interview is one of the circumstances to be considered under s 76(2)(b) of PACE (*R v Raghip* (1991)). In *R v Walker* (1998) it was held that nothing limits the form of mental or psychological condition on which a defendant can rely to show that his confession is unreliable.

But in *R v Coles* (1995) the Court of Appeal held that expert evidence is inadmissible to enable a jury to reach a decision about the existence of mens rea, *unless related to the mental health or psychiatric state of the defendant*. Thus, jurors have been held to be sufficiently acquainted with how ordinary people are likely to react to the stresses and strains of life (*R v Turner* (1975); but cf *Lowery v The Queen* (1974)). Similarly, they are not allowed to have expert evidence to tell them whether a person, not suffering from some defect or abnormality of mind, is likely to be telling the truth (*R v Mackenney* (1981)).

## Expert evidence on the 'ultimate issue'

Whether an expert could give his opinion on the ultimate issue, that is, the very question to be decided by the court, was a vexed question for a long time. So far as civil proceedings are concerned the question is now answered by s 3 of the Civil Evidence Act 1972, which provides that where a person is called as a witness in civil proceedings, his opinion on any relevant matter, including an issue in the proceedings, shall be admissible if he is qualified to give expert evidence on it.

In criminal cases evidence of an expert on a particular matter is sometimes excluded on the ground that it would be providing an opinion on the ultimate issue (see, for example, *R v Theodosi* (1993)). But the rule is frequently ignored. Thus, in *R v Stockwell* (1993) the Court of Appeal said that an expert is called to give his opinion and should be allowed to do so. What is important is that the judge should make it clear to the jury that they are not bound by an expert's opinion.

# 14 Privilege

This chapter and the next deal with reasons for excluding evidence that are unlike any previously encountered. Other exclusionary rules or principles have as the reason for their existence the need to secure a fair trial. The justification for the rules relating to privilege and public interest immunity has nothing to do with the fairness of the trial but with some other benefit that is thought to be more important. The rules about privilege and public interest immunity acknowledge that the public have interests that must occasionally be allowed to prevail over their interest in securing fair trials, at which all relevant and otherwise admissible evidence can be heard. Although these topics have this understanding in common, they operate differently. A *privilege* is a *right which the law gives to a person* allowing him to refuse to testify about a particular matter or to withhold a document. Effect is given to *public interest immunity* by means of a *power which the courts have* to exclude evidence on the ground that disclosure of information would be damaging to the general good.

There are three main privileges:

(a) privilege against self-incrimination;

(b) legal professional privilege;

(c) privilege arising from statements made 'without prejudice'.

## Privilege against self-incrimination

Section 14(1) of the Civil Evidence Act 1968, which is declaratory of the common law (*Rio Tinto Zinc Corpn v Westinghouse Electric Corpn* (1978)), describes this privilege as the right of a person in any legal proceedings, other than criminal proceedings, to refuse to answer any question or produce any document or thing if to do so would tend to expose that person to proceedings for an offence or for the recovery of a penalty. Section 14 extends the privilege in civil proceedings to protect a person's spouse. At common law the privilege was restricted to the person claiming it.

The privilege has to be claimed, on oath, by the person who wishes to rely on it. Thus, it cannot be claimed on discovery in a civil action by a solicitor on his client's behalf (*Downie v Coe* (1997)).

Statutes have abolished the privilege in certain cases. Sometimes that has been done by providing that a person may be questioned, but that only a limited use may be made of his answers (see, for example, s 31 of the Theft Act 1968; s 9 of the Criminal Damage Act 1971; s 98 of the Children Act 1989). At one time it was thought that the scope of the privilege could be cut down by the courts in a similar way but it is now accepted that where statute has not limited the use to which such evidence can be put, the civil courts have no power to impose a limit of their own devising (*Bishopsgate Investment Management Ltd v Maxwell* (1993)).

As well as cases where the privilege has been expressly removed by statute, there are cases where statutes have impliedly removed it. See, for example, *Re London United Investments plc* (1992) in relation to examinations under s 432 of the Companies Act 1985; *Bank of England v Riley* (1992) in relation to examinations under the Banking Act 1987; *Bishopsgate Investment Management Ltd v Maxwell* (1993) in relation to inquiries under s 235 or s 236 of the Insolvency Act 1986.

## Legal professional privilege

The scope of legal professional privilege at common law is reflected in s 10 of the Police and Criminal Evidence Act 1984 (*R v Central Criminal Court ex p Francis and Francis* (1988)). There are three categories set out in the Act.

### Section 10(1)(a) of PACE 1984

Communications between a professional legal adviser and his client or any person representing his client made in connection with the giving of legal advice to the client. Here the communication is a two-way system and can be thought of in the form of a straight line, with the client or his agent at one end and the legal adviser at the other. Thus:

Client/agent ◀——————————▶ Legal Adviser

The legal advice can be of any kind and does not have to be connected with litigation or the prospect of it. The protection is available even where the lawyer is an 'in-house' lawyer advising his employers (*Alfred Crompton Amusement Machines Ltd v Customs & Excise Commissioners* (1972)).

In *Balabel v Air India* (1988) Taylor LJ said that although the test for a privileged communication was whether it had been made confidentially for the purpose of obtaining legal advice, this purpose was not to be narrowly construed and should be taken to include practical advice about what should be done in the relevant legal context.

### Section 10(1)(b) of PACE 1984

Communications between lawyer, client *and third parties* for the purpose of pending or contemplated litigation. The lines of communication can be seen as forming a triangle so as to involve three parties instead of two. Thus:

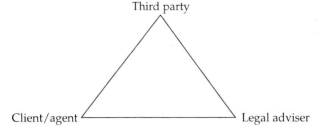

Third party

Client/agent                       Legal adviser

Here, the communications with the third parties, often other professionals such as surveyors, doctors or accountants, will be protected only if the dominant purpose is for use in litigation, pending or contemplated (*Waugh v British Rlys Board* (1980)).

### Section 10(1)(c) of PACE 1984

Items enclosed with or referred to in communications of types (a) or (b), provided the items came into existence in connection with the giving of legal advice and are in the possession of a person who is entitled to possession of them. The point here is that the privilege exists to protect communications between client, legal adviser and, sometimes, third parties. It does not exist to protect evidence from production (*R v King* (1983)).

Copies of original documents are frequently brought into existence in the course of a legal professional relationship. Whether their disclosure can be compelled depends on whether the *originals* would have been privileged or not. If the originals would not, the copies will not attract privilege just because they are part of a set of instructions to enable the client to obtain legal advice (*Dubai Bank v Galadari* (1989)).

Legal professional privilege will not protect a communication to facilitate crime or fraud. (*R v Cox and Railton* (1884); s 10(2) of PACE). 'Fraud' is very widely defined to include, in addition to the tort of deceit, 'all forms of fraud and dishonesty such as fraudulent breach of contract, fraudulent conspiracy, trickery and sham contrivances' (*Crescent Farm (Sidcup) Sports Ltd v Sterling Offices Ltd* (1972), *per* Goff J). This exception to the scope of legal professional privilege has more recently been expressed by saying that for the privilege to apply there must be 'absence of iniquity' (*Ventouris v Mountain* (1991), *per* Bingham LJ). In *Barclays Bank v Eustice* (1995) 'iniquity' was held to include obtaining advice about how to structure a series of transactions at an undervalue that would have had the effect of prejudicing the interests of creditors. The Court of Appeal held that it made no difference that neither the solicitor nor even the client realised that this would be the effect of what was proposed.

Experts' reports that are to be used at trial will have to be disclosed to the other party. But one party may obtain a report that he later decides not to use. Such a report will normally be covered by legal professional privilege. But there are two exceptions to this rule:

- reports from experts such as doctors and psychiatrists brought into existence by parties to cases involving the welfare of children. The overriding duty to regard the welfare of a child as paramount in such cases will not allow the parties to suppress 'unfavourable' reports (*Oxfordshire County Council v M* (1994));

- where an expert in his report refers to material that was supplied to him for the purpose of obtaining his opinion, any privilege attaching to that material will be waived when the expert's report is served on the other party. It makes no difference that the expert might have found the material unhelpful or irrelevant (*Clough v Tameside and Glossop Health Authority* (1998)).

### Duration of privilege

The general rule is, 'Once privileged, always privileged' (*Calcraft v Guest* (1898), *per* Lindley MR). So documents prepared for one action will continue to be privileged in subsequent litigation, even though the subject matter or the parties may be different. See, for example, *The Aegis Blaze* (1986). Another example of the maxim is the rule whereby documents concerning property rights that are privileged in the hands of one owner are privileged in the hands of that person's successors in title (*Minet v Morgan* (1873)).

It used to be thought that where the holder of a privilege could derive no further benefit from its exercise, the privilege could be defeated by the interest of another person who needed to have access to the information, particularly where this was needed to defeat a criminal charge. However, since the decision of the House of Lords in *R v Derby Magistrates ex p B* (1995), it is clear that this is not the case. The House of Lords said there that earlier decisions to the contrary had been wrong. It is a fundamental condition, on which the administration of justice rests, that a client must be sure that what he tells his lawyer will never be revealed without consent. Otherwise, the client might hold back half the truth.

### By-passing the privilege via secondary evidence

Legal professional privilege prevents facts *from having to be disclosed*. It does not prevent the facts *from being proved* if any other means of doing so can be found. Thus, in *Calcraft v*

*Guest* (1898), where the appellant had obtained copies of certain privileged documents and so was in a position to prove the contents of the originals by means of secondary evidence, the Court of Appeal held that he was entitled to do so.

It may be possible to block this escape route if the party who stands to lose the benefit of the privilege can obtain an injunction to restrain the use of the copies (*Ashburton v Pape* (1913)).

Although in *Ashburton v Pape* the remedy was granted on the basis of the court's power to protect confidentiality, in *Goddard v Nationwide Building Society* (1986), Nourse LJ took the view that the basis of relief was not the confidential nature of the communications, but the legal professional privilege attaching to them. The importance of this distinction may lie in the fact that, on the more recent view, there appears to be less scope for a judge to exercise his discretion when deciding whether to grant the injunction (see *Derby & Co Ltd v Weldon (No 8)* (1990)).

In *Butler v Board of Trade* (1971) it was held that public policy would prevent an injunction of this kind from being granted where its effect would be to restrain the prosecution from adducing admissible evidence in criminal proceedings, and in a case where the prosecution obtained a privileged communication by accident rather than impropriety, the Court of Appeal held that it could be used during the cross-examination of the defendant (*R v Tompkins* (1977)).

Although the privilege is that of the client, it may be waived by the solicitor as the client's agent *even though he may be acting under a mistake*. In particular, waiver may take place by accidentally disclosing privileged documents on discovery. Where this has happened and it is obvious that the other side has seen the document as the result of a mistake, this will not amount to waiver. But, if the person examining the privileged document might reasonably have concluded that the privilege was being waived, then it will have been lost (cf *Pizzey v Ford Motor Co Ltd* (1993) and *IBM Corpn v Phoenix (International) Computers Ltd* (1995)).

### 'Without prejudice' statements

This head of privilege is founded on the public policy of encouraging litigants to settle their differences. The rule applies to exclude from evidence all negotiations genuinely aimed at settlement, whether oral or in writing. Such statements are 'without prejudice' to their makers if the terms proposed are not accepted. The application of the rule does not depend on the use of the expression 'without prejudice', though it is safer to use it. If the circumstances make it clear that the parties were trying to settle a claim, evidence of the negotiations will not generally be admissible to establish an admission. Conversely, the use of the 'without prejudice' label will be of no effect where there is no attempt at settlement (*Re Daintrey ex p Holt* (1893)).

Evidence of negotiations will be admissible if it is necessary to show the terms of a settlement that was ultimately reached: for example, where one of the parties wants to sue on that agreement (*Tomlin v Standard Telephones and Cables Ltd* (1969)). But generally the without prejudice rule makes evidence of negotiations inadmissible in any subsequent litigation connected with the same subject matter, even where the parties are not identical (*Rush & Tomkins Ltd v GLC* (1989)).

# 15 Public interest immunity

Public interest immunity (PII), formerly called 'Crown privilege', is a rule of law that requires the withholding of documents on the ground that it would be harmful to the public interest to disclose them.

In *Duncan v Cammell Laird & Co Ltd* (1942) the House of Lords held that a court could not question a claim of Crown privilege, if made in proper form. It also said that claims to Crown privilege could be put on two alternative grounds:

(a) disclosure of the contents of the particular documents would harm the public interest, for example, by endangering national security or prejudicing diplomatic relations;

(b) the documents belonged to a class of documents that had to be withheld in the interests of 'the proper functioning of the public service'.

In 1956 Viscount Kilmuir LC, in a statement in the House of Lords, explained that the reason for claiming Crown privilege on a class, as opposed to a contents basis, was that it was needed to secure 'freedom and candour of communications with and within the public service', so that government decisions could be taken on the best advice and with the fullest information. People advising the Government must be able to know that they were doing so in confidence, and that any document containing their advice would not subsequently be disclosed.

The beginning of the modern approach to PII can be seen in *Conway v Rimmer* (1968), in which the House of Lords reversed its earlier ruling in *Duncan v Cammel Laird*, and held that in such cases it was for the court to decide where the balance of public interest lay: in protecting a government claim for secrecy, or in upholding a litigant's right to have all relevant materials available for the proper adjudication of his claim. But the idea that public interest immunity might be based on a class, rather than a contents, claim was still accepted.

PII can operate in cases not involving the government. In *R v Lewes JJ ex p Secretary of State for the Home Department* (1973) it was said that the old expression, 'Crown privilege', was wrong and misleading. While a minister was always an appropriate, and often the most appropriate, person to assert the public interest, it was open to any person to raise the question, and there might be cases where the trial judge himself should do so. So, for example, in *D v NSPCC* (1978) the House of Lords protected the anonymity of an informer who had reported suspicions of child cruelty to the NSPCC.

An important distinction between public interest immunity and the sort of privilege that might be claimed by a private litigant, such as legal professional privilege or the privilege against self-incrimination, used to be that a privilege might be waived, but a claim to public interest immunity could not. (See, for example, *Makanjuola v Commissioner of Metropolitan Police* (1992), *per* Bingham LJ.) This approach, coupled with a class claim rather than a contents claim, led to undesirably wide public interest immunity claims being made by ministers in a number of trials. The practice was criticised in the Scott Report (1996) and the central Government has now effectively abandoned class claims. In *R v Chief Constable of West Midlands Police ex p Wiley* (1995) the House of Lords held that a class claim cannot be made in respect of documents compiled as part of the investigation of a complaint against the police.

In recent decades the leading cases on PII in the House of Lords have been concerned with civil claims, and it is unclear whether the principles expressed in them are equally applicable in criminal trials.

The basic rule is that in public prosecutions witnesses may not be asked, and will not be allowed to disclose, the names of informers or the nature of the information given. The reason for the rule is that informers need to be protected, both for their own safety and to ensure that the supply of information about criminal activities does not dry up (*Marks v Beyfus* (1890)). This rule can be departed from if the disclosure of the name of the informant was necessary to show the defendant's innocence, but it is for the defendant to show that there is a good reason for disclosure (*R v Hennessey* (1978)).

The rule in *Marks v Beyfus* also protects the identity of persons who have allowed their premises to be used for police observation, as well as the identity of the premises from which observation was kept. Even if the defendant argues that identification of the premises is necessary to establish his innocence (because, for example, it has a bearing on the accuracy of witness observations), the judge may still refuse to allow the question to be put (*R v Johnson* (1989)). But the prosecution must first provide a proper evidential basis to support their claim for protection of identity. In *R v Johnson* Watkins LJ stated the following as minimum requirements:

- the police officer in charge of the observations must testify that he visited all the observation places to be used and ascertained the attitude of their occupiers, both as to the use to be made of them and to possible subsequent disclosure;

- a police officer of at least the rank of chief inspector must testify that immediately prior to the trial he visited the places used for observation and ascertained whether the occupiers were the same as when the observation took place and, whether they were or not, the attitude of those occupiers to possible disclosure of their use as observation points.

The object of keeping the identity of premises secret is to protect the owner or occupier. Where this consideration does not apply, cross-examination may be permitted on the details of surveillance (*R v Brown* (1987)).

A police informer may voluntarily sacrifice his anonymity, and PII cannot be used to prevent this (*Savage v Chief Constable of Hampshire* (1997)).

# 16 Facts not requiring proof

The general rule is that if a party wants to rely on a particular fact in support of his case, that fact must be formally proved by providing evidence of it at trial. To this rule there are two important exceptions:

(a) formal admissions;

(b) judicial notice.

## Formal admissions

### Civil trials

RSC Ord 27 r 1 provides that a party to a cause or matter may give notice 'by his pleading or otherwise in writing' that he admits the truth of the whole or any part of the case of any other party. Such formal admissions can be withdrawn only by leave of the court. Formal admissions may also be made and recorded on a summons for directions or pre-trial review.

Formal admissions may also be made in reply to a notice to admit facts. A party to a cause or matter may, not later than 21 days after the cause or matter is set down for trial, serve on any other party a notice requiring him to admit, for the purpose of that cause or matter only, such facts or such part of his case as may be specified in the notice (RSC Ord 27 r 2(1)). Answers to interrogatories may also constitute formal admissions (*AG v Gaskill* (1882)), and formal admissions may also be made through a party's advocate at trial.

**Criminal trials**

By s 10(1) of the Criminal Justice Act 1967:

- any fact of which oral evidence may be given in any criminal proceedings may be admitted for the purpose of those proceedings by or on behalf of the prosecutor or defendant;

- the admission of any such fact shall, as against the party making the admission, be conclusive evidence in those proceedings of the fact admitted.

By s 10(2) an admission under s 10(1) may be made before or at the proceedings, but if made otherwise than in court it must be in writing.

By s 10(3) an admission under this section for the purpose of proceedings relating to any matter shall be treated as an admission for the purpose of any subsequent criminal proceedings relating to that matter (including any appeal or retrial).

By s 10(4) an admission under this section may with the leave of the court be withdrawn in the proceedings for the purpose of which it is made or any subsequent criminal proceedings relating to the same matter.

A *Practice Direction* of 1995 provides that where there is a plea of not guilty at a plea and directions hearing, both prosecution and defence are expected to inform the court of facts which are to be admitted and which can be reduced into writing under s 10(2).

**Judicial notice**

'Judicial notice' refers to the acceptance by a judicial tribunal of the truth of a fact without formal proof, on the ground that it is within the knowledge of the tribunal itself.

Judicial notice may be applied to facts, which a judge can be called upon to accept:

- from his general knowledge of them (facts judicially noticed 'without inquiry');

- from inquiries to be made by him for his own information from sources to which it is proper for him to refer (facts judicially noticed 'after inquiry');

- by virtue of some statutory provision.

**Facts judicially noticed without inquiry**

These are facts that are regarded as matters of common knowledge. For example, in recent decades courts have taken judicial notice of the following facts:

- stripes are often used in football shirts to identify various teams (*Cook & Hurst's Design Application* (1979));

- Elvis Presley lived in the USA (*RCA Corpn v Pollard* (1982));

- postmen leave notices to the effect that a recorded delivery letter is being held for collection (*Hussein v Secretary of State for the Environment* (1984));

- temperatures fall at night (*Watts v Reigate and Banstead BC* (1984));

- more men than women leave surviving spouses (*Turner v The Labour Party* (1987));

- clearing banks in the UK usually charge compound, rather than simple, interest (*Bello v Barclays Bank plc* (1994));

- risky investments usually attract much higher rates of return than those with little risk attached (*IRC v Universities Superannuation Scheme Ltd* (1997)).

What is common knowledge differs according to time and place. For example, in *Calabar (Woolwich) Ltd v Tesco Stores* (1977) the Court of Appeal took the view that supermarkets were a recent and still growing development, and that courts could not take judicial notice of facts about them, but needed evidence.

**Facts judicially noticed after inquiry**

Whenever the meaning of words arises, however technical or obscure, then, unless there is some dispute about it, it is common practice for the court to inform itself by any means that is reliable and ready to hand. Counsel usually give any necessary explanation, or reference may be made to a dictionary (*Baldwin and Francis Ltd v Patents Appeal Tribunal* (1959)).

For the purposes of more complicated inquiries, reference may be made to such sources as reports of earlier cases, certificates from responsible officials, letters from Secretaries of State or statements made in court by counsel on their behalf, works of reference and the oral statements of witnesses. The cases show that such inquiries have generally been made in at least three types of case:

(a) where information is required about current political or diplomatic matters;

(b) about historical facts;

(c) about customs, including professional practices.

**Current political and diplomatic matters.**

If a court needs information about matters of this kind, it may formally ask a government minister to provide it. The answer will be regarded as conclusive in relation to the matters with which it deals (*Duff Development Co Ltd v Government of Kelantan* (1924)). Judicial notice has been used in determining:

- whether a foreign country was a sovereign independent state (*Duff Development Co Ltd v Government of Kelantan*);

- the extent of the UK monarch's territorial sovereignty (*The Fagernes* (1927));

- whether a person was entitled to diplomatic immunity (*Engelke v Musman* (1928));

- whether a state of war existed between the UK and a foreign state (*R v Bottrill ex p Kuechenmeister* (1947)).

**Historical facts**

It was held by the Judicial Committee of the Privy Council in *Read v Bishop of Lincoln* (1892) that when it is important to ascertain 'ancient facts of a public nature', the law permits historical works to be referred to.

The view was formerly taken that while judicial notice might be taken of facts of this nature, it would not extend to historical facts of a contemporary, or nearly contemporary kind. See, for example, *Commonwealth Shipping Representative v P & O Branch Service* (1923). But more recent decisions suggest that judicial knowledge may be taken of contemporary, or near contemporary, events. For example, judicial notice has been taken that:

- the invasion of Holland by the German army was in full swing during working hours on 10 May 1940 (*Cornelius v Banque Franco-Serbe* (1941));

- the American declaration of war against Japan took place in December 1941, and American forces began to arrive in the UK in working parties in 1942 (*R v Birkenhead Borough JJ ex p Smith* (1954));

- the Katyn massacre occurred (*Re St Luke's Chelsea* (1976));

- 1975 was an inflationary period when, in general, land values were rising rapidly (*Washington Development Corpn v Bamblings (Washington) Ltd* (1984));

- house sales and housing development were declining rapidly in England during 1990–92 (*Bovis Homes Ltd v Oakcliff Investment Corpn* (1994));

- there was currently religious conflict between Sikhs and Hindus in the Punjab (*Sandhu v Sandhu* (1986));

- there was currently a very turbulent political situation in Hebron *(Re A-R)* (1997)).

### Customs

Judicial notice may be taken of general customs that have been proved in earlier cases, despite the general rule that a court cannot treat a fact as proved on the basis of evidence heard in a previous case (*George v Davies* (1911)).

Judicial notice may also be taken of customs as a matter of general knowledge. For example, judicial notice has been taken of:

- the practice of the Ordnance Survey Office in compiling Ordnance Survey maps (*Davey v Harrow Corpn* (1958));

- the practice of the Comptroller General's Office in relation to applications for patents (*Alliance Flooring Co Ltd v Winsorflor Ltd* (1961));

- the practice of London solicitors in relation to company searches (*Re Garton (Western) Ltd* (1989)).

**Statutory provisions**

Several Acts of Parliament direct the courts to take judicial notice of various matters. For example:

- the Interpretation Act 1978 provides (re-enacting earlier provisions) that every Act passed after 1850 shall be a public Act and judicially noticed as such unless the contrary is expressly provided;

- by s 3(2) of the European Communities Act 1972 judicial notice is to be taken of various treaties, of the Official Journal of the Communities, and of any decision of, or expression of opinion by, the European Court on questions concerning the meaning or effect of any of the treaties or Community instruments.

There is no express provision for taking judicial notice of statutory instruments, but some have been so frequently relied on that judicial notice will be taken of them (*R v Jones* (1969)).

## Use of personal knowledge

While it seems clear that a tribunal may make use of its *general* knowledge by virtue of judicial notice, it is also said that neither judges nor jurors can make use of their purely personal knowledge in reaching a decision.

But the Divisional Court has on several occasions held that *magistrates* have properly applied their own knowledge of local conditions (*Ingram v Percival* (1969); *Paul v DPP* (1990)).

In *Wetherall v Harrison* (1976) the Divisional Court emphasised that although such special knowledge could be used to *interpret* the evidence given in court, it must not be used to *contradict* it. In *Bowman v DPP* (1990) it was said that justices must be extremely circumspect in using their own local knowledge. They should inform the parties if they are likely to use such knowledge, so as to give an opportunity for comment on the knowledge that they claim to have.

# 17 Judicial findings as evidence

The rule at common law is that a judicial finding in one case is inadmissible, in another case between different parties, to prove the facts on which the first decision was based. The reason for this is that it would be unjust for someone to have his rights affected by litigation to which he was not a party and in which, therefore, he could not be heard (*The Duchess of Kingston's Case* (1776)). But this principle was applied in such a way that criminal convictions had to be ignored in cases where common sense would have acknowledged them to be both relevant and weighty. Reform in civil cases was achieved by statute in 1968, and in criminal cases in 1984.

## Convictions as evidence in civil cases

At common law the effect of the rule in *Hollington v Hewthorn* (1943) was that in a civil trial, an earlier criminal conviction arising from the same facts was irrelevant, and therefore inadmissible.

The position was changed by the Civil Evidence Act 1968. By s 11(1), in any civil proceedings the fact that a person has been convicted of an offence by a UK court, or by a court martial in the UK or elsewhere, shall be admissible in evidence for the purpose of proving, where to do so is relevant to any issue in those proceedings, that he committed that offence.

By s 11(2), where a person is proved to have been convicted of an offence he shall be taken to have committed that offence unless the contrary is proved. But by s 13(1), in an action for libel or slander in which the question whether a person did or did not commit a criminal offence is relevant to an issue arising in the action, proof of the conviction is conclusive evidence that the person convicted committed that offence.

Because s 11(1) refers only to UK convictions, the rule in *Hollington v Hewthorn* continues to apply to convictions by foreign courts, and they therefore remain irrelevant, and so inadmissible (*Union Carbide Corporation v Naturin Ltd* (1987)). Nor does the section extend to adjudications of guilt in police disciplinary proceedings (*Thorpe v Chief Constable of the Greater Manchester Police* (1989)).

If a person has been convicted but there is an appeal pending, the court will not rely on the section. Instead, the civil hearing will be adjourned until the criminal appeal has been determined (*In re Raphael, decd* (1973)).

### The effect of s 11

There are two views about the effect of the section:

(a) the conviction itself has no weight as an item of evidence, but operates only as a trigger to activate the presumption under s 11(2) that the facts on which it was based are true;

(b) the conviction is in itself an item of evidence to be weighed in the scales against the defendant.

Both views can be found in the judgments of the Court of Appeal in *Stupple v Royal Insurance Co Ltd* (1971). Support for the second view can be found in *Hunter v Chief Constable of the West Midlands Police* (1982).

### Convictions as evidence in criminal cases

Some offences presuppose the commission of an earlier offence by someone else; for example, handling presupposes that the property handled has already been stolen. But at common law the earlier offence could not be proved by showing that someone had been convicted of it. The earlier conviction was regarded as no more than non-expert evidence of opinion, and so inadmissible (*R v Turner* (1832)). The law is now governed by s 74 of PACE 1984.

### Section 74 of PACE 1984

By sub-s (1), in any proceedings the fact that a person other than the accused has been convicted of an offence by any court in the UK shall be admissible in evidence for the purpose of proving, where to do so is relevant to any issue in those proceedings, that that person committed that offence.

By sub-s (2), where such evidence is adduced, that person shall be taken to have committed that offence unless the contrary is proved. Proof is to the civil standard, because that is the standard always applied where a defendant in a criminal case has the burden of proof in respect of any issue (*R v Carr-Briant* (1943)).

### The scope of s 74(1)

Clearly, proof of the commission of an earlier offence will be 'relevant to any issue' in the current proceedings if it establishes an element of the offence now charged. So, for example, in *R v Pigram* (1995), where two men were charged with handling stolen goods, the plea of guilty made by one of the defendants was held admissible at the trial of the other for the purpose of proving that the goods were stolen.

But the Court of Appeal has held that a wide interpretation should be applied to 'issue' so as to allow it to cover not just essential ingredients of an offence, but evidentiary matters also. In *R v Castle* (1989), evidence of the previous conviction, on his own plea of guilty, of someone who was no longer a defendant in the trial was held admissible to support a prosecution witness' evidence of identification.

While the Court of Appeal has said that it does not approve of allowing evidence to go before a jury that is irrelevant, inadmissible, prejudicial or unfair simply on the basis that is convenient for the jury to have 'the whole picture' (*R v Boyson* (1991)), it has also been said that 'anything which enables a jury better to understand the relevant factual background against which the issue arises is properly to be described as relevant to that issue within the terms of s 74.' So in a case where defendants were charged with conspiracy to pervert the course of justice by obtaining the false evidence of witnesses at an earlier trial, it was held proper to have proved that the earlier trial had resulted in a conviction, and that at a later trial others had already been convicted of conspiracy to pervert the course of justice in relation to the earlier trial (*R v Buckingham* (1993)). In *R v Warner* (1992) the defendants were charged with conspiracy to supply heroin. The prosecution case was based in part on police observations at the address of one of the defendants. These revealed that a great many people had visited the house. Eight of the visitors observed by the police had previous convictions for the possession or supply of heroin. The trial judge allowed evidence of these convictions to be adduced under s 74 and was upheld by the Court of Appeal. The previous convictions of the visitors were relevant to the characters of the people that the defendants were letting into the house, and this had a bearing on the nature of the transactions going on there.

**Interaction with s 78(1)**

Once a judge is satisfied that the evidence tendered under s 74(1) has some probative force, careful consideration should be given to s 78(1) to see whether the discretion to exclude should be exercised (*R v Boyson* (1991)).

In several cases (for example, *R v Kempster* (1989)), the Court of Appeal has suggested that the discretion to exclude ought to be exercised where the earlier conviction was obtained as the result of a guilty plea, rather than a contested trial. But the court has not always taken this view. See, for example, *R v Grey* (1988); *R v Turner* (1991).

It has been said that the sub-section should be 'sparingly' used (*R v Robertson* (1987)) and in *Warner v Jones* (1988) it was suggested that it might have been wiser not to use it since it added little to an already strong case against the defendants.

It has also been said that where the evidence that the prosecution wish to adduce under s 74(1) expressly or by necessary inference imports the complicity of the person on trial in the offence with which he is charged, the sub-section should not be used (*R v Kempster* (1989)). The cases on conspiracy show that in that area this principle is likely to be applied. In *R v O'Connor* (1987), a case in which conspiracy between only two persons was alleged, the Court of Appeal held that the trial judge should have used s 78(1) to exclude evidence of the co-accused's conviction (cf *R v Robertson* (1987), where the conspiracy was alleged to have been between the defendant, two other named men, and other unknown persons. The Court of Appeal held that evidence of the convictions of the other named men had been rightly admitted).

### Evidence of previous acquittals

Evidence of previous acquittals will only rarely be admitted in either civil or criminal proceedings. The reason is that the different standards of proof in civil and criminal cases will usually have the effect of making a defendant's previous acquittal on a criminal charge irrelevant in subsequent civil proceedings arising from the same facts. It remains the case that even where what amounts to a serious crime is alleged, the standard in civil proceedings is proof on a balance of probabilities (*Re H* (1996)).

In criminal proceedings a previous acquittal remains subject to the rule in *Hollington v Hewthorn*: it is irrelevant and inadmissible (*Hui Chi-Ming v The Queen* (1992)).

But a previous acquittal will be admissible if it is possible to argue that it is relevant to any of the issues that the court has to decide, and sometimes a court will be satisfied that it is relevant to an issue of credibility (*R v Cooke* (1987)). A previous acquittal may also become relevant if it is connected to a previous conviction to which the prosecution wish to refer (*R v Doosti* (1985)).

# 18 Documentary evidence

A party who wishes to rely on a statement contained in a document as evidence supporting his case needs to consider, in addition to any other relevant evidence law, at least one further matter: proof of the contents of the document. In some cases, proof of due execution may have to be considered also.

So far as criminal cases are concerned, the basic provisions are contained in the Criminal Justice Act 1988, as amended. This provides:

- where a statement contained in a document is admissible as evidence in criminal proceedings, it may be proved either by the production of that document, or, whether or not the document is still in existence, by the production of a copy (s 27);

- a 'statement' is any representation of fact, however made; a 'document' is anything in which information of any description is recorded; and a 'copy', in relation to a document, is anything onto which information recorded in the document has been copied, by whatever means and whether directly or indirectly (Sched 2, para 5);

- a copy may be authenticated in such manner as the court may approve. It is immaterial how many removes there are between a copy and the original (s 27).

Since the Civil Evidence Act 1995 has provisions in the same terms (ss 8 and 13), proof of the contents of a document is now essentially the same in both civil and criminal proceedings. Where a copy is produced, the courts appear to have a wide discretion as to the manner in which it may be authenticated, but the best method is likely to be proof by the evidence of a person with custody and control of the copy that it is a true copy of the original.

NB: that where an original document is not available, s 27 of the Criminal Justice Act 1988 and s 8 of the Civil Evidence Act 1995 do not go so far as to allow proof of the contents of the original by oral evidence. At this point there remains a divergence between civil and criminal evidence law. In civil proceedings, although s 8 of the 1995 Act does not sanction the admission of oral evidence, oral hearsay evidence of the contents of a document that would itself be admissible if it were available can be given under the general provision for the admission of hearsay evidence contained in s 1 of the Act.

But in criminal proceedings the admissibility of oral evidence of the contents of a document is governed by common law. The basic common law rule is that only primary evidence of the contents of a document (that is, the original document itself) is admissible. There are three relevant exceptions:

(a) *Destruction or loss of original*
    Destruction by fire was one of the earliest acceptable excuses for failure to produce an original (*Leyfield's Case* (1611)), and the principle was afterwards extended to cover other circumstances in which the original had been lost or destroyed (*Blackie v Pidding* (1848)). Before the exception can be applied where a document is missing, proof must be given that an adequate search has been made (*Brewster v Sewell* (1820)).

(b) *Other impossibility or inconvenience*
    Production of a document may be excused, and secondary evidence given of its contents, when it is impossible for reasons other than destruction or loss to

EVIDENCE

produce it, or even when it would be highly inconvenient to do so. Thus secondary evidence can be admitted of writing on a wall and of an inscription on a tombstone (*Mortimer v M'Callan* (1840)). Similarly, secondary evidence has been admitted of:

- inscriptions on flags and banners (*R v Hunt* (1820));

- the contents of a placard on a wall (*Bruce v Nicolopulo* (1855));

- the contents of a document in the custody of a foreign court (*Alivon v Furnival* (1834));

- the contents of a notice that was required by statute to be fixed permanently to a wall (*Owner v Bee Hive Spinning Co Ltd* (1914)).

(c) *Lawful non-production by a stranger*
Secondary evidence will be admissible where a stranger to the litigation lawfully declines to produce a document in his possession or control. (A witness with no such justification can, in theory, be compelled to produce a document at trial by a witness summons.) Thus, secondary evidence has been given of the contents of a document where:

- the original was unavailable because of privilege (*Mills v Oddy* (1834));

- the document was in the possession of a stranger outside the jurisdiction (*Kilgour v Owen* (1889));

- the document was in the possession of a person entitled to diplomatic immunity (*R v Nowaz* (1976)).

The party who adduces a document in evidence must usually, in the absence of an admission by his opponent, prove that it was duly executed. This obligation may simply require evidence that the document was signed by the person whose signature it purports to bear. Sometimes it may be necessary to prove the handwriting of the whole of a disputed document. Proof of execution may also require proof of attestation.

Proof of a signature or of handwriting may be made in one or more of the following ways:

- by evidence of the writer, or of someone else who saw the maker of the document write it or put his signature on it;

- by evidence of opinion, given by an ordinary witness. Such evidence is admissible even where the evidence of the writer is available. Thus, on a charge of forgery, it is not *necessary* to call the person whose signature is alleged to have been forged (*R v Hurley* (1843));

- by an actual comparison, often aided by expert opinion evidence. Section 8 of the Criminal Procedure Act 1865 applies to both civil and criminal proceedings and provides that comparison of a disputed writing with any writing proved to the satisfaction of the judge to be genuine shall be permitted to be made by witnesses; and such writings, and the evidence of witnesses respecting the same, may be submitted to the court and jury as evidence of the genuineness or otherwise of the writing in dispute.

In civil proceedings, the judge has to be satisfied on the balance of probabilities as to the genuineness of the writing that is to be used as a standard for comparison. In criminal proceedings, he must be satisfied beyond reasonable doubt (*R v Ewing* (1983)).

The Criminal Procedure Act 1865 does not expressly *require* the evidence of witnesses. Once a document has been proved to the judge's satisfaction to be a genuine sample of handwriting from the person who is alleged to have written the disputed document, it may apparently simply be compared with the disputed document by the jury. But it has been held that in criminal cases expert evidence should also be available (*R v Harden* (1963)).

'Attestation' refers to the signature of a document by a person who is not a party to it, but who is a witness to the signature of one of the parties. By s 3 of the Evidence Act 1938, any document required by law to be attested, with the exception of a will or other testamentary document, 'may, instead of being approved by an attesting witness, be proved in the manner in which it might be proved if no attesting witness were alive'. The effect of this provision is that non-testamentary documents required by law to be attested may now be proved by showing that the signature is in fact that of the attesting witness.

Where the court is asked to pronounce for a will in solemn form, the general practice is for at least one of the attesting witnesses to be called to give evidence of execution. But a will can be pronounced for where both attesting witnesses are proved to be dead, or even if the evidence shows merely that they cannot be traced, if the court is satisfied in all the circumstances that the will was duly executed (*Re Lemon's Estate* (1961)).

In any proceedings, proof of execution may be dispensed with in the case of 'ancient documents', which, by s 4 of the Evidence Act 1938, are documents more than 20 years old. For this rule to apply, the document must appear to be regular on the face of it, and must be produced from proper custody. 'Proper custody' is any custody that is consistent with the genuineness and legitimate origin of the document (*Bishop of Meath v Marquess of Winchester* (1836)).

## Statements in documents produced by computers

There are no special rules in civil proceedings. In criminal cases the law is governed by s 69 of PACE 1984.

Section 69 is aimed at establishing the reliability of the computer evidence. It provides that a document produced by a computer shall not be admissible as evidence of any fact stated in the document unless it is shown that:

- the computer was not being improperly used so as to affect the accuracy of the statement;

- the computer was operating properly.

The word 'computer' was not defined in the 1984 Act. Whether the document is original or hearsay evidence, the conditions in s 69 must be satisfied by evidence (*R v Shephard* (1993)).

If there is a contested issue, the court must hold a trial within a trial to decide whether the party wishing to rely on the document has established a foundation for doing so under s 69. The ordinary standards of proof apply: if the prosecution want to produce the document, they must establish the existence of the conditions beyond reasonable doubt; if the defence want to produce the document, they need establish the conditions only on a balance of probabilities (*R v Minors* (1989)).

A person wishing to produce computer evidence cannot rely on a presumption that the computer is working properly. Reliability of the computer evidence as required by s 69 can be proved by tendering a written certificate, or by oral evidence (Sched 3, paras 8 and 9 of PACE). But only malfunctions that affect the way in which the computer processes, stores or retrieves the information used to produce the statement are relevant (*Reid v DPP* (1998)). It is also necessary for the computer records themselves to be produced to the court (*Burr v DPP* (1996)).

When a certificate is relied on, it must show on its face that it is signed by a person who, from his or her job description, can confidently be expected to be in a position to give reliable evidence about the operation of the computer. In most cases it will be possible to discharge the burden by calling a witness who is familiar with the operation of the computer, in the sense of knowing what the computer is required to do, and who can say that it is doing it properly (*R v Shephard* (1993)).

Even if a certificate is tendered, the court may require oral evidence of the matters that could otherwise be proved by the certificate (Sched 3, para 9 of PACE). However, this evidence may itself be hearsay (*R v Neville* (1991)).

# 19 Real evidence

'Real evidence' is an ill-defined concept. There is general agreement that it includes physical objects produced for the inspection of the court. If a document is adduced in evidence, the question whether it is 'real' or 'documentary' evidence depends on the purpose for which it is adduced. If the purpose is to establish its contents, it is classed as an item of documentary evidence; if the purpose is to establish its condition or appearance it is classed as an item of real evidence. 'Real evidence' has also been held to include the following items.

### Physical appearance of a person or animal in court

In *Line v Taylor* (1862) a dog was brought into court to display its good temper. Before defendants in criminal trials were allowed to give evidence, the jury might take into account their reactions in the dock at various stages of the trial (*AG for New South Wales v Bertrand* (1867)). The demeanour of a witness has traditionally been regarded as relevant to credibility (*Teper v R* (1952)). The resemblance of a child, produced to the court, to a person alleged to be its father has been held to be some evidence of parentage (*C v C and C* (1972)).

### Views

Things and places outside court may be inspected during the course of a trial. In *Buckingham v Daily News Ltd* (1956) the Court of Appeal held that such an inspection was part of the evidence in the case. The parties, their legal representatives and the judge (or judge and jury) should all be present at the view (*R v Ely JJ ex p Burgess* (1992)).

### Automatic recordings

Where the recording device operates as no more than a calculator, the printout or other reading is an item of real evidence; for example, the printout produced by a breathalyser (*Castle v Cross* (1984)). In *R v Spiby* (1990) the Court of Appeal had to consider whether the rule against hearsay applied to the printout from a device which monitored telephone calls and recorded the numbers to which calls were made and their duration. The court held that the printout was an item of real evidence and not caught by the hearsay rule, because the recording was entirely automatic and did not depend on anything that had passed through a human mind.

The contents of tape recordings may be admitted as evidence of what was said on a particular occasion (*R v Maqsud Ali* (1966)).

The voices recorded must be identified by admissible evidence, but it is enough merely to establish a *prima facie* case for authenticity (*R v Robson and Harris* (1972)). Such a recording is a document within the meaning of s 27 of the Criminal Justice Act 1988, and a transcript of the recording will be admissible as a copy under the same section.

In *R v Rampling* (1987) the Court of Appeal gave the following guidance on the use in court of tape recordings of police interviews:

- the tape can be produced and proved by the interviewing officer or any other officer present when it was taken;

- the officer should have listened to the tape before the trial so that he can, if necessary, deal with any objections to authenticity or accuracy;

- the transcript of the recording can be produced by the officer. He should have checked this against the recording for accuracy before the trial;

- the defendant is entitled to have any part of the tape played to the jury;

- if any part of the tape is played, it is for the judge to decide whether the jury should have a transcript to enable them to follow more clearly.

Subject to any necessary editing to remove inadmissible evidence, a jury in retirement may, on request, be allowed to hear a tape recording of a police interview with the defendant, where the tape has been made an exhibit, even though the tape has not been played earlier during the trial (*R v Riaz and Burke* (1991)). Any playing of the tape after the jury has retired should be in open court, with judge, counsel and the defendant present (*R v Hagan* (1997)).

A jury may also want after retirement to see once again a video tape of an interview with a child made under s 32(A) of the Criminal Justice Act 1988. It is a matter for the judge's discretion whether this should happen. If there is a replay, the following rules apply (see *R v Rawlings and Broadbent* (1995)):

- it must be in court, with judge, counsel and defendant present;

- the judge should warn the jury that because they are hearing the evidence-in-chief of the complainant a second time, well after all the other evidence, they should guard against the risk of giving it disproportionate weight simply for that reason, and should bear well in mind the other evidence in the case;

- to assist in maintaining a fair balance, when the video has been replayed the judge should remind the jury from his own notes of the cross-examination and re-examination of the complainant, whether the jury ask him to do so or not.

In *R v Morris* (1998) the Court of Appeal said that the transcript of a child's evidence-in-chief, given by way of video interview, should only rarely remain with the jury when they have retired to consider their verdict. In those rare cases the judge must warn the jury against giving it disproportionate weight.

A film or photograph may be admitted to prove the commission of an offence and the identity of the offender. For example, in *R v Dodson* (1984) photographs taken by a security camera at a building society office were held admissible to show an offence being committed. Films or photographs are treated as if they are extensions of human perception. In *Taylor v Chief Constable of Cheshire* (1986) police officers saw a video recording made by a security camera of someone picking up an item in a shop and putting it in his jacket. The police identified the man as the defendant. The film was later accidentally erased, but the Court of Appeal held that the officers' evidence of what they had seen on the tape had been properly admitted because they were in effect in the position of bystanders who had witnessed the event.

# 20 Estoppel

## Statement of the rule

An 'estoppel' exists when, in consequence of some previous act or statement to which he is a party, a person is precluded from afterwards showing the existence of a different state of affairs than that indicated by the previous act or statement.

The rule is based on considerations of justice and public policy. It would be *unjust* to allow someone to do or say something, yet afterwards try to obtain an advantage by denying the validity of what he did earlier, or the truth of what he said earlier. It would be *contrary to public policy* to allow identical claims to be repeatedly litigated.

But estoppel cannot be used to authorise illegality. Thus if powers that are *ultra vires* are assumed by a person or body, estoppel cannot be used to authorise what has been done (*Ministry of Agriculture and Fisheries v Matthews* (1950)).

Estoppel may apply where the act or statement is that of someone who is a 'privy' of one of the parties to the litigation in question. A 'privy' is someone who has a special type of legal connection to someone else, for example, for some purposes an agent is the privy of his principal, and vice versa.

For the purposes of evidence law, estoppel can be divided into three types:

(a) estoppel by previous judicial proceedings;

(b) estoppel by deed;

(c) estoppel by representation.

## Estoppel by previous judicial proceedings

A judgment is conclusive against everyone in relation to the legal state of affairs that it produces. This is of special importance where the judgment affects the status of a person or thing (a 'judgment *in rem*'), for example, a judgment to the effect that a person is divorced, or that a ship seized in wartime is not a neutral vessel.

A judgment also has the effect of preventing the parties to an action, or their privies, from *denying the facts on which it is based*. This form of estoppel may operate either as 'cause of action estoppel' or as 'issue estoppel', and is based on two policy considerations:

(a) litigation should be final;

(b) nobody should be harassed twice in respect of the same cause of action.

See *Carl Zeiss Stiftung v Rayner and Keeler Ltd (No 2)* (1967).

### Cause of action estoppel

Cause of action estoppel applies only when the cause of action in the earlier proceedings is identical to that in the later proceedings (*Buehler AG v Chronos Richardson Ltd* (1998)). It prevents a party to an action from asserting or denying, as against the other party, the existence of a particular cause of action, the existence of which has already been determined in a final judgment on the merits in previous litigation between the same parties. If judgment was given for the plaintiff in the earlier action, the cause of action no longer exists (and so cannot be sued on again) because the judgment has taken its place. If judgment was given for the defendant in the earlier action, the effect is that the earlier court has found the cause of action not to exist.

As a result, the unsuccessful plaintiff can no longer assert that it does.

Originally, this form of estoppel was known as 'estoppel by record' (the record being that of the court delivering the judgment), but it is now immaterial whether the judicial decision has been pronounced by a tribunal that is required to keep a written record of its decisions or not (*Carl Zeiss Stiftung v Rayner and Keeler Ltd (No 2)* (1967)).

A final judgment 'on the merits' means a judgment on the cause of action that cannot be varied, re-opened or set aside by the court delivering it, or by any other court of equal jurisdiction, although it may be subject to appeal to a court of higher jurisdiction (*The Sennar (No 2)* (1985)).

There will be no judgment on the merits when an action is dismissed for want of prosecution (*In re Orrell Colliery and Fire-Brick Co* (1879)). But default judgments and judgments by consent are treated as judgments 'on the merits' (*Kok Hoong v Leong Cheong Kweng Mines Ltd* (1964)).

A judgment obtained by fraud or collusion will not give rise to an estoppel (*The Duchess of Kingston's Case* (1776)).

### Issue estoppel
Issue estoppel can arise in circumstances where the causes of action are not the same. There are many causes of action that can be established only by proving that two or more different conditions are fulfilled. Such causes of action involve as many separate issues between the parties as there are conditions to be fulfilled by the plaintiff in order to establish his cause of action. If, in litigation on one cause of action, any of the separate issues as to whether a particular condition has been fulfilled is determined by a court of

competent jurisdiction, neither party can, in subsequent litigation between one another on any cause of action that depends on the fulfilment of the identical condition, assert that the condition was fulfilled if the court in the first action determined that it was not. Nor can either party subsequently deny that such a condition was fulfilled if the court in the first action determined that it was. (*Thoday v Thoday* (1964)).

For issue estoppel to apply, three conditions must be satisfied:

(a) the same issue must have been decided in the earlier case;

(b) the judicial decision in the earlier case must have been final;

(c) the parties to the decision, or their privies, must be the same persons as the parties to the proceedings in which the estoppel is raised, or their privies.

See *Carl Zeiss Stiftung v Rayner and Keeler Ltd (No 2)* (1967).

Issue estoppel, like cause of action estoppel, is a feature of adversarial procedure. Where proceedings have an inquisitorial element, therefore, issue estoppel will not be strictly applied. So, for example, issue estoppel could rarely, if ever, apply to proceedings for divorce, or to children's cases (*In re B* (1997)).

Under the rule in *Henderson v Henderson* (1843), issue estoppel has been extended to cover not only the case where a particular point has been raised and specifically determined in the earlier proceedings, but also the case where a party later attempts to raise a point that might have been, but was not, raised in the earlier proceedings. This is founded on the principle of public policy in preventing multiplicity of actions (*Talbot v Berkshire County Council* (1994)).

But for the rule in *Henderson v Henderson* to apply, the parties to the earlier decision must not only have been the same persons as the parties to the later action in which the estoppel is raised. They must also be suing or being sued in the later action in the *same capacities* as in the first (*Marginson v Blackburn Borough Council* (1939); *C (A Minor) v Hackney London Borough Council* (1996)).

Where the first judgment was obtained by default, the rule in *Henderson v Henderson* is unlikely to be applied (*Arnold v National Westminster Bank plc* (1991)).

### Discovery of new evidence

The general rule is that a party who has been unsuccessful in litigation will not be allowed to re-open that litigation unless the new evidence entirely changes an aspect of the case, and it could not by reasonable diligence have been discovered before (*Phosphate Sewage Co Ltd v Molleson* (1879)). In *Arnold v National Westminster Bank plc* Lord Keith suggested that it should be easier to overcome an issue estoppel than a cause of action estoppel where a party relies on further relevant material which he could not by reasonable diligence have adduced in the earlier proceedings.

## Analogous provisions in criminal proceedings

In criminal law the pleas of autrefois acquit and autrefois convict are available to prevent a defendant's being put in what is sometimes called 'double jeopardy'. In *Connelly v DPP* (1964) Lord Morris laid down these propositions:

- a man cannot be tried for a crime in respect of which he has previously been acquitted or convicted;

- a man cannot be tried for a crime in respect of which he could on some previous indictment have been convicted;

- the same rule applies if the crime in respect of which he is being charged is in effect the same, or substantially the same, as a crime in respect of which he has been acquitted, or could have been convicted, or has been convicted;

- one test as to whether the rule applies is whether the evidence that is necessary to support the second indictment, or whether the facts that constitute the second offence, would have been sufficient to procure a conviction on the first indictment, either in relation to the offence charged, or in relation to an offence of which, on that indictment, the accused could have been found guilty.

A substantial inroad on the common law has been made in ss 54–57 of the Criminal Procedure and Investigations Act 1996. These sections introduce the concept of 'tainted acquittals' and apply to acquittals in respect of offences alleged to have been committed on or after 15 April 1997.

The provisions apply where (a) a person has been acquitted of an offence, and (b) a person has been convicted of an 'administration of justice offence' involving interference with or intimidation of a juror or a witness, or potential witness, in any proceedings that led to the acquittal (s 54(1)).

Where it appears to the court before which the person was convicted that there is a real possibility that, but for the interference or intimidation, the acquitted person would not have been acquitted, the court shall certify that it so appears, unless it would be contrary to the interests of justice to take proceedings against the acquitted person for the offence of which he was acquitted, whether because of lapse of time, or for any other reason (ss 54(2) and (5)).

Where a court has certified under these provisions, an application may be made to the High Court for an order quashing the acquittal. Where such an order is made, proceedings may be taken against the acquitted person for the offence in respect of which he was acquitted.

By s 55, the High Court shall not make an order quashing an acquittal unless four conditions are satisfied:

(a) it appears to the High Court likely that, but for the interference or intimidation, the acquitted person would not have been acquitted;

(b) it does not appear to the court that, because of lapse of time or for any other reason, it would be contrary to the interests of justice to take proceedings against the acquitted person for the offence of which he was acquitted;

(c) it appears to the court that the acquitted person has been given a reasonable opportunity to make written representations to the court;

(d) it appears to the court that the conviction for the administration of justice offence will stand. In determining whether this condition is satisfied, the court shall take into account all the information before it, but shall ignore the possibility of new factors coming to light.

There is no equivalent of issue estoppel in criminal proceedings (*DPP v Humphrys* (1977)).

## Estoppel by deed

Where an action is brought on a deed, the parties to the deed and those claiming through them, such as successors in title, are estopped from denying the truth of the facts stated in the deed (*Bowman v Taylor* (1834)).

Whether recitals in a deed bind all the parties is a matter of construction in each case (*Greer v Kettle* (1938)).

Estoppel by deed will not operate so as to prevent a party from relying on fraud, duress, illegality, or any other fact entitling him to rescission or rectification of the deed (*Greer v Kettle* (1938)).

## Estoppel by conduct

An estoppel may arise where it would be unconscionable for a person to deny a representation of fact that is implicit in his conduct. Such an estoppel may arise from:

- agreement;
- express or implied representation;
- negligence.

For there to be estoppel by conduct, the representation must relate to an existing fact and be unambiguous.

### Agreement

A person may not deny the title to land of someone to whom he has paid rent for that land (*Cooke v Loxley* (1792)). Nor may bailees, licensees and agents deny the title of their bailors, licensors or principals after having effectively acknowledged them in the transactions carried out on their behalf (*Gosling v Birnie* (1831); *Crossley v Dixon* (1863)).

### Express or implied representation

Where a person by words or conduct wilfully causes another to believe in a certain state of things, and thereby induces him to act or to alter his own previous position, the representor will be estopped from alleging that a different state of affairs existed at the time when the representation was made (*Pickard v Sears* (1837); *Greenwood v Martins Bank Ltd* (1933)).

### Negligence

To establish estoppel by negligence, it has to be proved that a duty of care was owed to the person who has suffered loss and that there has been a breach of that duty (*Coventry, Sheppard & Co v Great Eastern Rly* (1883); *Mercantile Bank of India Ltd v Central Bank of India Ltd* (1938)).